CONCILIUM

Religion in the Eighties

CONCILIUM

Editorial Directors

General Secretariat: Prins Bernhardstraat 2, 6521 AB Nijmegen, The Netherlands

Concilium 205 (5/1989): Sociology of Religion

CONCILIUM

List of Members

Advisory Committee: Sociology of Religion

SPORT

Edited by
Gregory Baum
and
John Coleman

English Language Editor
Philip Hillyer

T & T CLARK
Edinburgh

October 1989
ISBN: 0 567 30085 4

ISSN: 0010-5236

Typeset by C. R. Barber & Partners (Highlands) Ltd, Fort William
Printed by Page Brothers (Norwich) Ltd

Concilium: Published February, April, June, August, October, December.
Subscriptions 1989: UK: £29.95 (including postage and packing); USA: US$49.95 (including air mail postage and packing); Canada: Canadian$64.95 (including air mail postage and packing); other countries: £29.95 (including postage and packing).

Contents

INTERNATIONAL CONGRESS FOR THEOLOGY

ON THE THRESHOLD OF THE THIRD MILLENNIUM

TUESDAY EVENING, SEPTEMBER 11, 1990

Panel Discussion: Present Situation of Theology in the World

Theologians from different continents and cultures will report on the present situation of theology in the Church in their countries.

The introductions will be followed by a general discussion to give members and observers a chance to exchange their opinions in a plenary session.

CONCILIUM 205 Special Column

Leonardo Boff

Anti-communism: End of an Industry

REAL SOCIALISM is undergoing undeniable changes affecting the foundations of socialist structures. It is enough to cite a few instances which have become symbolic: glasnost *and* perestroika *in the USSR, modernisation in China, rectification in Cuba. There is also the recognition of religion as a basic anthropological datum, extremely important for the construction of a human society which has room for generosity, gratuitousness, the moral sense of existence and the proper cultivation of utopia (all expressions used by Kharchev, the Soviet leader responsible for religious affairs), the frequent use in Gorbachev's statements of the expression 'spirituality' to denote the importance of intersubjectivity and the irreplaceable value of the individual as a human being.*

Perhaps the most important fact was the meeting on 11 June 1988 between the then Soviet President, Andrei Gromyko, with Patriarch Pimen at a reception in the Supreme Soviet for 500 religious authorities who had come from all over the world to celebrate the millennium of Christianity in the lands of Rus. For more than two hours there was an open debate between the audience and Gromyko on religious issues, disarmament and collaboration between the churches for world peace. These facts, and many similar, cannot be interpreted perversely as if it were all just another atheist trick to ridicule religion as an opium. In the heart of the Kremlin something was, and still is, changing. I believe that the correct interpretation of such facts is as an indication of substantial changes in the conception of socialism. The Stalinist version, dogmatic and authoritarian, seems to have been definitively superseded. Even though the repression in China tries to smother the demands for greater freedom, the mass demonstrations in the

Square of Heavenly Peace and the victory of Solidarity in Poland remain facts, attempts to increase democratic spaces within socialism without, as some Western groups wrongly interpret them, abandoning the socialist road as a route to a more human society.

What do these few facts show? They show that there are no forms of absolutism either in the churches or in societies which resist for long the ideals of citizen participation in political life. These are the most ancient political ideals of the human race, and they always win through against all obstacles of repression or control.

These facts also reveal that the industry of anti-communism has its days numbered. Powerful sectors of society connected with the university/industrial/military complex used to live on the confrontation between communism and capitalism. On the communist side was oppression, on the capitalist democracy. Today we find that the countries of the East enjoy hegemony in the discourse of democracy while oppression increases in the peripheral and dependent capitalist countries. It is now clearer that the basic question is not the confrontation between East and West, between capitalism and communism, but between North and South, between developed countries and countries kept in underdevelopment. What are the capitalist and socialist systems doing to pull two-thirds of the human race out of degrading poverty? What are they doing together to avoid a nuclear apocalypse over everything created and everything constructed by the immense effort of humankind?

Finally, the churches are now relieved of the social function assigned to them by bourgeois-liberal Western governments, keeping anti-communism alive under the pretext of defending religion and human freedoms. Today communism is becoming open to a positive recognition of the religious dimension in human beings, and is proposing a democracy which is more total than the bourgeois form because it is based on the revolution against hunger already achieved and consolidated, something which has not occurred in the Western democracies, which coexist with large bands of poverty within the rich countries and dozens of poor and degraded countries as their satellites.

That the churches can change is shown in exemplary fashion by John-Paul II's Sollicitudo Rei Socialis. *In the face of the urgent threats to humanity's survival, we must break out of our slavery to opposing systems in order to join together to* build solidarity; *more than an ethical virtue, it is a political value, the only one capable of guaranteeing peace and the continuation of life on earth. To think in this way is to have already moved beyond capitalism and real socialism. Only solidarity at all levels will be able to make us, not sons and daughters of necessity, but sons and daughters of happiness in a human race finally reconciled with itself and with creation.*

Translated by Francis McDonagh.

Note that this Special Column, like others in this series, is written under the sole responsibility of the author.

SPORT

Editorial: Sport, Society and Religion

IF ONE pays any attention to the news media at all, it would be almost impossible to overestimate the importance and impact of sport on modern society. Four years ago international newspaper headlines screamed out, '39 Dead in Heysel', the result of soccer hooliganism and abuse of alcohol at a stadium near Brussels. As a consequence, British soccer teams were barred from matches on the continent for a probationary period.

Few modern phenomena elicit such intense attraction and emotional bonding as sports. The star athlete becomes a representative icon and sport teams serve as surrogates for intense local or nationalistic loyalties. As the Yale University philosopher Paul Weiss notes in his excellent study, *Sport: A Philosophic Inquiry*, 'Both when participated in and when watched, sport quickly works on the emotions; it wins men's allegiance readily and often to a degree nothing else is able to do. Mankind's enthusiasm and devotion to it is remarkable and deserves to be remarked upon.' P. S. Frederickson observes, 'There is no society known to man which does not have games of the sort in which individuals set up purely artificial obstacles and get satisfaction from overcoming them.'[1] Art, science, and philosophy, surely, make larger contributions to civilisation than sport does. Agriculture, manufacture and business play a much larger role in our economy than would be possible to sport, though, of course, sport is not without its economic importance. But, rarely do these other human enterprises 'enter into men's daily disputes or lay claim to basic loyalties in the way or to the degree that sport does. It is sport that catches the interest and elicits the devotion of both young and old, the wise and the foolish, the educated and the uneducated.'[2]

3

In 1969, in the famous 'football war', El Salvador and Honduras even went to war with each other over a disputed soccer match! Some have seen in sport a useful catharsis for innate human aggressive instincts, a kind of moral equivalent of war. Others note a propensity for irrational emotional bonding at large sport events which leads, at times, to the kind of riots we witnessed in Amsterdam in the spring of 1989 after a match pitting the intense rivals, Ajax of Amsterdam and Feyenoord of Rotterdam, against each other. Coming on the heels of the tragic deaths of ninety-four fans crushed to death in Sheffield, England, the Amsterdam riots sowed new doubts about any inevitably humane potential in sport.

It is also frequently claimed that sport builds human character and tests it, on a small scale, to prepare for larger tests and crises in life. It is also urged that sport promotes and improves international goodwill. Yet news stories about the illegal use by athletes of drugs and steroids (a Canadian Olympic star was stripped of his medal at the Seoul Olympic games for illegal use of drugs) or gambling scandals involving pay-offs to 'throw' a game (The American baseball star, Pete Rose, now manager of the Cincinatti Reds, is presently under investigation for gambling irregularities) raise serious questions about any inevitable nexus between sport and building character. As for goodwill, Paul Weiss states the point apodictically. 'There is no evidence that sport, itself, on a national or international scale, helps promote even elementary goodwill.'[3]

Some readers may be surprised that a *Concilium* issue on sociology of religion treats of sport. Yet the editors are convinced that Max Scheler's words of over sixty years ago still hold true. 'Scarcely an international phenomenon of the day deserves social and psychological study to the degree that sport does. Sport has grown immeasurably in scope and in social importance, but the meaning of sport has received little in the way of serious attention.'[4]

To be sure, since the mid-1960s and, accelerating in this last decade, the scholarly literature in sociology of sport has proliferated in many countries (*e.g.* Jeffre Dumazedier in France; Eric Dunning in England; Gunter Erbach in Germany; Gregory Stone and Harry Edwards in the USA). Since 1968, the International Committee on the sociology of sport (an affiliate of UNESCO) has held bi-annual congresses, probing issues of sport and society. New social histories are being written about the rise of mass sports in France, England, and the United States. In West Germany and the Soviet Union sociology of sport flourishes. But one looks almost in vain for any more serious spiritual and theological assessment of this important topic. This we attempt to begin in this volume.

The editors feel very strongly that sport represents an important human good. Sport constitutes an anthropological universal. It is found in almost every known human society. Sport involves both contest and play. For the participating athlete, it represents a test of bodily excellence, speed, endurance, strength, accuracy, co-ordination, skill and gracefulness. Our human love for skilled exertion, movement and bodily grace, our delight in stretching the human boundaries and in spontaneity, our intense interest in the drama of sport contests—these embodied, almost erotic, qualities lend to sport its capacity for human excellence and delight. For the spectator, sport provides aesthetic pleasure, bonding between fans and team, human diversion in watching a game where skill and chance merge to form a human drama. As Allan Guttmann notes in his excellent book, *From Ritual to Record*, sport provides a kind of ecstasis from the mundane. 'In sport we can discover the euphoric sense of wholeness, autonomy and potency which is often denied us in the dreary rounds of routinized work that are the fate of most men and women.'[5]

The editors also feel strongly that the original and emancipatory potential of sport as an arena of human bodily excellence, skilled competition and play needs to be accented and retrieved against distortions of sport by over-commercialisation, racism, sexism and class bias. So this issue of *Concilium* treats of sport *and* society as well as sport *in* society (the latter recognising an autonomous element to sport). Assuredly, structured games mirror a structured society.

We know from sociological evidence that the kinds and range of sports played vary with the social class of the participants. The poor and working-class lack access (and money to provide the needed equipment) to polo, golf, tennis, skiing, sailing, even, frequently, swimming. We also know that the higher the educational level of a strata in society, the greater is its level of *active* sports participation.[6] But we should not exaggerate. There is, perhaps, less alienation in modern sport—whatever its deformations— than elsewhere in the modern world. Sport may approximate more to the ideal of a merocratic social order than any other sphere of social life. Our purposes, then, are in no way to debunk sport.

Besides class bias, sport reflects racist and sexist attitudes in the host society. Racism is strongly reflected in the organisation of sport in South Africa and raises questions about boycotting teams who play in that country. Racism still infects organised sport in the United States where Negro athletes are rarely promoted to managers and coaches of teams, although they are now given equal access to participate as athletes. Unfortunately, an earlier commissioned article dealing explicitly with racism and sport fell through at the last minute. Luckily, Roberto DaMatta's intriguing article on soccer in Brazil touches on this sensitive theme of racism and sport.

We should not imagine that there is a direct continuity between modern sports and the ancient Greek ideal and practice of sport. It is quite clear that the rise of our modern organised sports coincides with the rise of industrialism. Allan Guttman, drawing on Max Weber, lists seven traits of modern sports which differentiate them from ancient Greco-Roman or medieval sports:

(1) *Secularism*: the original nexus between sport and religious festivals and feast days has been broken. Moreover, an earlier large involvement by the Christian Churches in sponsoring sport teams has declined in the industrialised nations.

(2) *Equality of opportunity to compete and in the conditions of competition*: the ancient Olympic games were not open at all, certainly not to women. Many medieval games, *e.g.* jousting, were restricted to the nobility. Alcibiades could despise organised gymnastics because 'athletes were of low birth, inhabitants of petty states and of mean education'.[7] Equality of opportunity as an ideal is one of the great achievements of modern sports, even when it fails completely to realise that ideal.

(3) *A specialisation of roles*: modern organised sports have become professional and very specialised. They employ trained coaches, paid players who are frequently restricted to one role, *e.g.* goalie in soccer or forward in basketball. The role of the amateur, unique in the ancient and medieval world, now gives way to professional sport stars.

(4) *Rationalisation*: modern sports are rule-bound and teams are rationalised into leagues, following set schedules, employing referees, following clear patterns of franchise-ownership and career mobility for athletes, etc.

(5) *Bureaucratic organisation*

(6) *Quantification*: this goal eluded the ancients who lacked stop watches, photo equipment, calculation machines for statistics, etc.

(7) *Governed by the quest for records*: the ancients knew winners and losers of races but not breakers of records. Preoccupation with record-breaking reflects a mechanical obsession.

In short, something of a Weberian disenchantment of sports has occurred in modernity. But some of the bonds between religion and sports remain.

In the Anglican cathedral of St John the Divine in New York City, a stain-glassed window depicts players of American baseball and other modern sports. Indeed, a few theologians have even postulated the notion of a *Deus Ludens* (a God who plays) to ground a connection between God and the games.[8]

Put briefly, modern sport spectacles can function, sometimes, as an alternative form of religion. Sport represents, like religion, an appeal to ritual. Ceremony inaugurates a sporting event (a bugle is sounded, a flag raised, an anthem sung) to represent a break from mundane, profane time and space. Like religious ritual, sport presents us with a bounded time-space field. As Michael Real puts it, speaking of American football, 'Sports overlie the sacred cycle of mythic time to provide a needed psychic relief from the tedium of western linear time.'[9] Jürgen Moltmann warns us, in his article in this issue, against the dangers of a false religion of sport. But sport can also take on a religious meaning that is authentic. The articles by Sean Freyne, Thomas Ryan and Hans Lenk probe this dimension of sport. As Paul Weiss has noted, 'As the Bhagavad-Gita long ago affirmed, the man of action, once he has detached himself from the pragmatic import of his efforts, achieves what the contemplative does, once he has turned his mind away from contingencies to dwell on that which is forever. By a distinct route the athlete, too, can arrive at the result the yogi seeks.'[10]

This volume is divided into three main sections. Part I treats of sport and society. Klaus Heinemann raises the main questions about how sport can give us information about what is going on is society with political relevance but which cannot be easily analysed in formal socio-political terms. John Coleman focuses on the interplay of sport and ideology, sketches a map of the evolution of sport in modern society and treats of the discourse used to justify sport in modern society. Gunter Pilz treats the important issue of sport and violence and shows how working-class and unemployed youth find in soccer a sense of meaning denied them elsewhere. Nancy Shinabarger traces the theme of sexism in sports and shows how a feminist re-appropriation of the sport ideal includes an emancipatory interest.

Part II, Sport and National Culture, contains two case studies which explore sport's reinforcing of a Durkheimian solidarity with locality. Sport feeds into patriotism and reflects the social dramas and contradictions of the culture. Roberto DaMatta's brilliant article about soccer in Brazil uncovers what is unique about Brazilian soccer and how it mirrors the national themes of chance and destiny. Bruce Kidd's study explores the ways capitalist and commercial forms of sport distort the original ideals of Canada's national game, hockey.

Part III is called Sport: Ethics and Religion. In this section Dietmar Mieth links sport to the ethical themes of justice and solidarity and proposes a model of discernment to adjudicate between humanising and less authentic forms of sport. Sean Freyne draws out the earliest Christian reactions to sport to conclude: 'There is nothing in the authentic Christian tradition that is negative to sport as such, but there is much there to warn us to be constantly critical of its abuse.' Jürgen Moltmann's study of the Olympic ideals of a *religio-athleticae* warns against the dangerous idea of sport as religion. The final two essays show us a spiritual dimension in sport. Thomas Ryan views sport as a discipline of body awareness which plays into and supports a contemplative attitude. Hans Lenk speaks of the Zen of sport.

This issue of *Concilium*, then, looks at sport to raise issues about the authentically religious use of sport versus the idolatrous or inhumane in sport, about sport as an arena of human excellence versus the forces which draw that excellence down to mediocrity or distortions. In the final analysis, the editors pose the question: if sport is *in* society as a major social force, in what ways does it reflect the distorted face of our societies, in what ways can it help to emancipate our social life together before and under God?

Gregory Baum
John Coleman

Notes

1. P. S. Frederickson, 'Sports and the Cultures of Man' in Warren Johnson, ed., *Science and Medicine of Exercise and Sports* (New York 1960), p. 634.
2. Paul Weiss, *Sport: A Philosophic Inquiry* (London 1969), p. 9.
3. Weiss, *Sport*, p. 143.
4. Max Scheler, 'Introduction' in Alfred Peters, *Psychologie des Sports* (Leipzig 1927), p. xii.
5. Allen Guttman, *From Ritual to Record* (New York 1978), p. 157.
6. On class and sport, *cf.* Gunther Luschen, 'Social Stratification and Social Mobility Among Young Sportsmen' in John Loy and Gerald Kenyon, eds., *Sport, Culture, Society* (New York 1969), pp. 258–276.
7. Isocrates, Loeb Classical Library, vol. III (Cambridge 1961), p. 27.
8. *Cf.* Eugen Fink, *Spiel als Weltsymbol* (Stuttgart 1966) and David Miller, *Gods and Games* (New York 1969).
9. Michael Real, 'SuperBowl: Mythic Spectacle', *Journal of Communications* 25 (1975), s. 35.
10. Weiss, *Sport*, p. 244.

PART I

Sport and Society

Klaus Heinemann

Sport and Society: The Major Questions

1. The development and present state of the sociology of sport

THE SOCIOLOGY of sport is the discipline primarily concerned with investigating the connections between sport and society. It is a relatively young science. It was only in the second half of the 1960s that the sociology of sport developed into an independent area of research and teaching, first in the United States and then in a number of West European countries, especially Great Britain, Finland and West Germany. Nonetheless the scope and intensity of academic efforts to investigate sport with sociological techniques have increased rapidly in recent years, with the result that there is now a well-developed sociology of sport also in Belgium, Canada, France, East Germany, Japan, Poland and the USSR.[1] As the discipline has developed, particular national focuses have emerged. In West Germany sport organisations (sporting clubs and associations and commercial sport promoters) have been much studied. French sociology of sport discovered very quickly the close connection between sport, economy and politics. In Great Britain in particular there are significant works on sport, violence and spectator disturbances. Finland has become known for studies on the connection between sport and the cultural value system. United States scholars focused at an early stage on the problem of racial discrimination in sport, problems of professionalisation and sport with ethnic minorities. Socialist countries belonged to a dogmatically ideological academic tradition influenced by Marxism and consequently followed a social philosophy approach, and were less open to empirical study; though here too, particularly in recent times there have been empirical studies on sport and life-style and sport and physical culture.[2] In Western industrial countries there was a discussion in the sport sociology of the first half of the 1970s on the position and dependence of sport in (capitalist) societies. A sport critique influenced by the so-called Frankfurt School, partly neo-Marxist in approach, has attempted to describe sport as an element of class society or of a late capitalist society.

The variety of topics studied and research conclusions produced in this period makes it impossible to give anything like a complete survey of the field.

2. Sport and society

The first area of sociological investigation of sport covers the various forms of dependence of sport on cultural value systems and features of social structure. This study makes it clear that sport cannot be understood purely in its own terms, as a natural phenomenon. In this connection the main contribution comes from studies on the connection between sport, the human body and society. Sport is one structured way of relating to the body and consequently social value-judgments, interpretations and rules concerned with the body play a crucial role in the understanding of sport and willingness to engage in sport, and of the significance sport has for individual identity. Attitudes to physical contact, modesty and pain thresholds, health ideals, the nature of expressive physical controls, and the image of the body as these are regulated in a society have an enormous influence on ability and willingness to practise sport or a particular sport.

The connection between sport and society is also made in the various views put forward about the evident parallelism of development between, on the one hand, the spread of sport, its differentiation into so many branches, its growing popularity and the development of a strong organisation and, on the other hand, the development of a modern industrial society. The central argument is that under the conditions of industrial labour the energy demand on our bodies is no longer sufficiently high, and at the same time in industrial production the individual has become an anonymous, replaceable cog, receiving no respect or recognition as a person. Sport develops as a possibility whereby the individual can compensate for these deficits experienced in the world of industrial labour.

Other factors in the close connection between sport and society include the following:
(a) Never before have people had so much time for themselves as in our modern industrial societies. Working time, whether measured by the average working week, the average working year or working life, is steadily

decreasing, while average life expectancy is increasing. People are less and less defined and burdened by the conditions and demands of their professions or by the world of work. Parallel with this increase in our free time runs an increasing affluence, which is what creates the freedom to take advantage of the various possible uses of this increasing free time.

Leisure time and sport are increasingly becoming individual interests independent of the constraints of work. These possibilities derive not only from the fact that we enjoy a steadily increasing amount of free time, but primarily because technical improvements have so far reduced workplace stress that there is a steadily decreasing demand on the individual's mental and physical energies, and leisure time loses the function of restoring the energy needed for work or compensating for the negative experiences of work or profession. This enables individuals to cut themselves off from work outside the workplace much sooner, to gain access to new areas of activity and experiences, and to exploit these newly acquired areas of activity independently. In this way sport and play can be, as it were, disconnected from the demands of work and the world of utilitarian calculations.

(b) It is against this background of the expansion of individual freedom of choice that we have to interpret developments such as individualisation and differentiation of life-styles. Existing social behaviour patterns, often associated with membership of a particular social stratum, a professional group or sex and age characteristics, are losing their binding force; religion, tradition, family and work are losing their function of providing meaning. This leads to a variety of changes and upheavals in the individual's situation. Individuals are left much more to themselves in the shaping of their lives and status; they can develop their identities according to their own ideas and needs. This development becomes visible in the variety and diversity of life-styles and forms of self-realisation, particularly in the area of leisure, which is the first area in which experience-based forms of identity definition are sought. The more freedom of choice available to an individual, the greater the emphasis on expression of individual needs, the implementation of one's own ideas, according to one's own interests, on freedom from ties and obligations and on spontaneity and self-fulfilment.

This is reflected, for example, in the increased demand for forms of play, sport and movement in which rules are less important, a development most clearly seen in 'never-never games', that is games which, because of their lack of detailed rules, because of the creativity and spontaneity they require in the sequence of movements and the variability of social relationships, can only be played once, that is, cannot be repeated in the same form, and certainly not as a competition. They are played in non-standard spaces with constantly new implements. In them the role of the trainer also changes, as there is a shift towards the idea of the facilitator.

(c) Sociological studies on the loss of values in our society indicate a decline in the importance of performance as a goal or motivation. Particularly people in service occupations, with high school and college qualifications, seem to be rejecting the conventional performance ethic. A consequence of this is that performance as a goal in sport, the maximising of physical competence through long-term training, loses attractiveness. At the same time, however, sport is becoming popular for age-groups and social classes which do not see maximal performance and competition as the main attraction of sport.

(d) The quest for health, physical fitness and an attractive appearance is becoming increasingly important for those groups of people aged 30 and over who are discovering or rediscovering sport. The selling of sport through the use of the ideal of health, combined with the fact that physical fitness, endurance and an attractive physical appearance are increasingly regarded as good in themselves and with an increasing awareness of the role of prevention in health care, is encouraging a growing demand for 'healthy' forms of movement—particularly in the middle and higher age groups.

3. Sport as a social system

The second area of research in the sociology of sport consists of the social structures and processes of sport.

For a long time teams and other groups in sport were the main focus of academic interest. In addition to formal structures and positions, the sociology of sport must pay attention to the additional informal and partly spontaneous codes of behaviour, such as the allocation of tasks (goalmaker or core defender in ball games and similar), the working out of strategy (e.g. in doubles in tennis), pacemakers for colleagues in a team or club (as in races). Other issues studied in this connection are conflicts, structures of domination and interest, leadership styles in different teams and types of sport and the influence of these on sporting performance and on identification with the group.

Studies on sporting organisations have a particular importance in sociological research into sport. These studies concentrate mainly on the organisation of the club, that is, with the characteristics of voluntary associations. They have produced data of fundamental importance on the structure of club membership, active involvement in sport, willingness to take part in social events, on decision-making within the club, and the function of sports clubs for their members. There are also statements about their organisational and financial structure, their facilities, on the problems of honorary and full-time officials. Other topics investigated are processes of bureaucratisation, that is, the increasing codification of rules, differentiation of roles and clear connections between functions and responsibilities and behaviour patterns in sport, as well as professionalisation and commercialisation.

Increasing attention is being paid in sociological research to the position and importance of honorary officials in clubs, because they have a crucial importance for the sport in the organisation of the club and also have great theoretical importance in relation to efficiency, tendencies to professionalisation, career models, selection and the absorptive capacity of the organisation.

The most recent development in the field has been the growth of new forms of sport organisation: fitness centres, gym studios, sport schools and leisure parks are providing increasing competition for sports clubs and associations. Holiday companies and resorts have found sport an attractive element of their package. Sport is being called on to fulfil an increasing number of therapeutic functions, and is gaining access to rehabilitation centres, spas and therapy groups. Marketing and sport management companies are becoming increasingly important in the organisation and marketing of sport and in the organisation of competitions. Churches, political parties, parishes, universities, organisations of commercial sports promoters, tour operators and the media are increasingly discovering sport as a way to make their 'core programme' more attractive. The organisational structure of these promoters and the nature and staging of the sport in question are accordingly attracting increasing attention in the literature of the sociology of sport.

4. Social figures in sport

A fairly large number of studies in the sociology of sport can be grouped under the heading 'social figures in sport'. These studies focus primarily on specific groups of people in sport with respect to their:
  – social origin, life and career;
  – particular role situations and action problems;
  – structure of motivation and reasons for being involved in sport.
This is numerically the largest number of studies in the sociology of sport, which makes it difficult to give a comprehensive overview; instead we shall present the most noteworthy conclusions.

(a) The motivation and structural characteristics of sport practitioners

Particular attention is being devoted to the motivation and social structure of those who practise sport. The main sociological interest in this topic is in the fact that the composition of the group is totally unrepresentative of the national population. All the studies show, in fact, that younger people engage in sport more often than older, and members of upper and middle social classes more often than those of lower social classes, and lower-class sport enthusiasts are interested in different types of sport from their counterparts in the middle and upper classes. It also appears that the participation of women in sport is much less than that of men, at least within the same social class. Finally, there are sports which are seen as typically male, and others generally regarded as more suited to the female 'nature'. A further element is the role played by religious affiliation in sporting activity. All studies confirm that involvement in sport in Western industrial countries is greater among Protestants than Catholics, though it is unclear whether these differences are the result of different forms of socialisation and different attitudes to achievement in different religious communities, or of the fact that Protestants are over-represented in middle and upper social classes and in urban areas, and so have more possibilities of practising sport.

Profound changes have been noted in recent years in the composition of the active sporting population, mainly in the direction of increasing differentiation. New groups are constantly coming to sport: elderly people, people with disabilities, ethnic minorities, lower social groups, women. Each group brings its own competence, its own attitude to achievement, its own motivation and its own degree of willingness to be involved in a club, leading to a fragmentation of the sport according to different expectations and types of motivation. These new groups are not just a reflection of changes in our population structure; they are more significant as an expression of new social problems: single people, adults with the particular worries and burdens of their work, people approaching retirement, couples whose children have grown up, elderly and often lonely people, in other words people who look to sport for positive support and emotional and social bonds.

These changes have clear consequences. The motives of those who engage in sport, the elements the individual seeks in sport, are becoming more diverse, and increasingly receive an individual stamp, become an expression and component of an individual life-style. The striving to improve performance and match it in competition with that of others is no longer the sole motivation of interest in sport, as sport becomes attractive for age

groups and social classes for whom maximising performance and competition are not its main attraction. There is a more active search for forms of play, sport and movement which are not structured by disciplined training with a long-term aim of improving performance, but depend on a different and often more varied cluster of motives.

(b) High performers

Surveys with appropriate questions are also being carried out among high-performance athletes. Latterly questions have increasingly been raised about the mental and social stress of young high-performing athletes, as the problems of competitive sport among children have become more prominent in public discussion.

(c) Fans

Mainly because of the violent disturbances associated with (football) matches, fans have been the object of a number of empirical studies. These studies have shown that the typical fan does not exist. Fans form a heterogeneous group, combining supporters, young people dressed in club colours, enthusiasts, organised and 'wildcat' fans, young people in search of sensation or carnival excitement and a number of young people with criminal tendencies. This work also provides information about the world of these young people, their family and work situation, their ties with social groups, their physical appearance and their degree of control over reality, and about rituals used to create group identity, support their team and engage in clashes with the police.

(d) Trainers and coaches

In addition to participants, active and passive, various studies have also investigated the social figure of the trainer. These studies have clarified the responsibilities, activities, qualifications and working conditions of trainers, and also looked at the structural characteristics of the role. Trainers are handicapped by the openness of their situation, in which they are the objects of high expectation but have no clearly defined role, and have to reconcile for themselves the expectations of the different groups to which they relate.

5. Social processes in sport

Alongside social structures, in which the sociology of sport devotes particular attention to the ways in which sport is organised, a further important area of research for the sociology of sport is the description of social processes, that is events and changes within given social structures. The sociology of sport has devoted particular attention to two processes, socialisation and aggressive or violent behaviour. I shall give more detail of some of the main findings of studies of this topic.

(a) Socialisation in sport

Socialisation has occupied a large place in the sociology of sport partly because, by virtue of the position and function of sports studies in general, it is closely connected with the training of sports teachers. Accordingly, particular attention is given to the effects of sport on personality and behaviour. It has the further aim of providing a critique of the frequently very general statements made about the socialising function of sport. Studies on this subject fall into two groups. One follows a more theoretical approach, deriving from work done on socialisation in general, and examines the conditions and possibilities of socialisation in sport. The other starts from empirical investigations into the measurable effects of socialisation.

An inspection of the literature indicates, first, that the concept of socialisation is used in a markedly diffuse and ambiguous way, and that ideas and expectations about the possible socialising effects of sport vary widely. As a result, nothing can be said about the socialising effect of sport in general. There is also an established division into 'presocialisation', that is, those processes which lead to sport and prepare for it, socialisation in sport, and finally the transfer of socialisation into other areas of life. The underlying question here is the extent to which changes mediated through sport are stable and can be effective in other areas of life. The overall view of the socialising effects of sport is pessimistic, mainly because of the competing effects and influences in sport, and because negative as well as positive effects may be associated with sport, and only in the individual case is it possible, taking into account the surrounding conditions and structural factors in the individual case, to discover which socialisation effects in the end prevail.

(b) Violence and aggression in sport

Study of the causes and allied factors involved in aggressive actions by players covers structural features, such as may derive from the rules of the sport, situational influences such as the state of the game (findings from research by Gabler), the behaviour of the referee or umpire, the nature and place of the rule infringement, individual dispositions, and the interaction between violence among spectators and violence among players. Other studies provide information on problems and factors of spectator aggression and on the behavioural patterns, lives and backgrounds of fans. In this connection a particularly important group of studies deals with the presentation of aggression and violence in the mass media.

Although the sociology of sport has developed rapidly in recent years, the state of knowledge attained is still regarded as unsatisfactory. For example, there are no theories capable of providing appropriate and unified explanations of the diversity of sport and of behaviour in sport. Far too little investigation has been carried out into the many consequences of high-performance sport, with its problems of commercialisation and professionalisation. Nor does sufficient importance seem to have been attached hitherto to the relationship between sport and politics. And finally there is need for research into future developments in sport and sporting interests.

Translated by Francis McDonagh

Notes

1. An indication of this is the various introductions and collections published about sport in different countries: see Bibliography.
2. This summary can only be a very crude reflection of the diversity of research in various countries. There is a very good survey of the sociology of sport in different countries in two special issues of the *International Review for the Sociology of Sport*, 22/1 (1987) and 24/1 (1989).

Bibliography

Claeys, U., *sport-en* . . . (Louvain 1986).
Ferrando, M. G., *Deporte y Sociedad; Las Bases Sociales del Deporte en España* (Madrid 1984).
Heinemann, F., *Einführung in die Soziologie des Sports* (Schorndorf 1983).
Heinilä, K., *Urheilu—ihimen—yhteiskunta* (Sport, Individual, Society) (Jyväskylä 1974).
Jue, B., *Analyse du sport* (Paris 1987).
Kuczynski, J., 'Play as negation and creation of the world', *Dialectics and Humanism* II, I (1984).
Loy, J., McPherson, B., and Kenyon, G. S., *Sport and Social Systems* (Reading, Mass. 1978).

Lüschen, G., and Sage, G. H., *Handbook of Social Sciences of Sport* (Champaign, Ill., 1981).

Olin, K., ed, 'The Contribution of Sociology to the Study of Sport', *Festschrift K. Heinilä* (Jyväskylä 1984).

Parlebas, P., *Eléments de Sociologie du Sport* (Paris 1986).

Rigauer, B., *Sportsoziologie* (Reinbek 1982).

Snyder, E., and Spreitzer, E., *Social Aspects of Sport* (Englewood Cliffs, NJ, 1983).

John Coleman

Sport and the Contradictions of Society

FOR SOME readers, perhaps, the title of this essay will seem puzzling. Is not sport, precisely, a universal trait, rooted strongly in what Friedrich Schiller called a universal play-impulse (*Spiel-trieb*)? Should not sport draw us on to transcend class, culture, national boundaries and the various social contradictions of society? And yet critics of sport such as Theodore Adorno can speak of 'bourgeois sports' and others extol a 'socialist' sport untainted by what they decry as the excessive individualism ('the star system') and competitive impulse of capitalist sport.

To be sure, sport and play are anthropological universals, found in some form in every culture and society. But they also always and everywhere reflect—as any other cultural formation—the basic contradictions of their own society.

Robert J. Higgs has distinguished between sport (hunting and fishing, for example), sports (physical games of competition), physical education (which need not be competitive as, for example, nautilus training or jogging) and play—of which sport is a sub set. But play also includes non-sport such as word games, card games, popular dancing, some forms of choral singing, etc. Drawing on some distinctions of Roger Callois in his book, *Les Jeux et les Hommes*, Higgs suggests that we define sport as a species of *agon* (struggle). He defines sports 'as competitive games that are bound by rules in space and time, thus differing from other forms of play in this regard, and requiring strain or agony, both mental and physical, on the part of contestants'.[1]

In this article, I will pose four major questions: (1) Why must sport reflect the contradictions of society? (2) How has sport evolved in the modern,

Western industrialised societies and what contradictions does this evolution show? (3) How does sport reflect the competing ideologies of modernity: bourgeois liberal, fascist and Marxist? (4) What are the dominant models of discourse in Western society at present for talking about sport and its meaning? Finally, in a concluding remark I will suggest some reasons why religion must be concerned about sport as it reflects the contradictions of society.

1. Why sport reflects the contradictions of society

I have already evoked the terms 'competitive' and *agon* in the definition of sport. These terms alone should alert the reader that sport can be caught up in the larger struggle for power and hegemony in society. British sociologist, John Hargreaves, picks up this theme. He notes that there is not only unequal access (both as participants and spectators) to sport but 'the differential capacity of dominant and subordinate groups to create appropriate discourses and develop appropriate strategies in relation to the uses of free time and the significance they accord to sporting activity'.[2] For, in modern society sport represents more than the spontaneous eruption of playful energy. Sport is sponsored and underwritten by businesses, inculcated in schools, regulated by sports commissions and even overseen by the state itself. Agencies of society allocate monies for sport and determine whether budgets reflect sports for all or only sports for an athletic elite.

The American economist, Thorsten Veblen, in his classic study, *The Theory of the Leisure Class*, contends that the *agon* of sport becomes an arena for the playing out of the *agon* of class interests. 'Sport is a kind of class instrument, serving to protect and disseminate upper class interests and values', Veblen claims. No one, perhaps, has better caught the reason why sport (but, note, the same is true of sexuality, religion, the intellectual life) is never, in the concrete, value-free, never a simple human good untainted by the contradictions of society, than John M. Hoberman in his book, *Sport and Political Ideology*.

> Sport is a latently political issue in any society, since the cultural themes which inhere in a sport culture are potentially ideological in a political sense. This latent political content becomes more evident when one considers some major polarities which bear on sport and the political world: amateurism vs. professionalism, individualism vs. collectivism, male supremacy vs. feminism, nationalism vs. internationalism, sensationalism vs. hygienism. All of these thematic conflicts belong to

the world of sport, and all are of ideological significance in the larger sense.[3]

The Nazi sports theorist Alfred Baemler could postulate: *Der Lieb ist ein politicum*—the body is a political instrument. Without endorsing, of course, his particular use and meaning for this maxim, I agree with the statement. Over and over again, sport is called upon to serve as an index of public health. Are our people flabby, unvigorous, enervated? Return to sport! Do we succeed in international sports competitions? It demonstrates the public health of the nation!

A deep debate has ranged among theorists of sport about the question of which takes precedence; work or sport/play. When Ortega y Gasset wrote about sport in his essay, 'The Sportive Origin of the State', he took a decidedly polemical stance against the labour theories of Marx. 'If the classic instance of the obligatory effort which strictly satisfies a need is found in what man calls work', wrote Ortega y Gasset, 'the other, the effort *ex abundantia cordis*, becomes most manifest in sport. We thus feel called upon to invert the inveterate hierarchy. Sportive activity seems to us the foremost and creative, the most exalted, serious and important part of life while labor ranks second as its derivative and precipitate.'[4]

We can contrast this position of Ortega y Gasset with two Soviet sport sociologists who write. 'Certain western sociologists try to view leisure as a complete distancing of man from work, as something opposed to work. We cannot agree with such ideas. Leisure in a communist society is not a fleeing from work but one of the transitional forms to a truly communist form of work, at which point the latter becomes enjoyment and the primary vital need.'[5]

Much is at stake, ideologically, in this seemingly arcane debate about the priority of work over sport or *vice versa*. Are humans to be defined more by their desires and aspirations or their needs? Were people created ultimately to work or to play? Play and sport, in particular, originated in sacred festivals and continued throughout much of recorded history to have religious connotations and connections. Sport draws beyond itself to a sacred grounding. At least, so argued J. H. Huizinga in his classic book, *Homo Ludens*.[6] The myth of a primordial character to play is rooted in the notion of divinity. 'With a word whose depth surpasses all logical understanding,' writes Huizinga, 'Plato once called men the playthings of the gods. Today one might say that man everywhere uses the world as his plaything.'[7]

Sport inexorably points to discipline, competition, body-narcissism (sport as display) and sexuality. Sport almost never represents (as a total societal complex as opposed to a given game) a neutral, a-political social and personal good. This is not to say that sport does not contain an emancipatory human potential or that it cannot be a genuine human good. I violently disagree with Theodore Adorno when he writes, 'Sports belong to the realm of unfreedom, no matter where they are organised.'[8] Intellectuals, such as Adorno, sometimes forget they have bodies! My point is more direct. Only a critical reflection on sport as it is actually organised will uncover the many ways it reflects the latent contradictions of society (sexism, racism, class contradictions, the consumer culture, etc.). Only such a critical reflection, with a deep emancipatory interest in recovering its human potential, will keep sport from reinforcing these contradictions of society. The *ludique* becomes the *tragique* if we do not aim at a critical retrieval of its original emancipatory purposes of human excellence, dwelling in and through the body in play, and a meritocracy of competition among equals.

2. The evolution of sport in modern, industrialised societies

There exist, to be sure, important historical differences in the path of the evolution of sport in various countries in the West, *e.g.* the pre-eminence of gymnastics in the German-speaking countries connected with the nineteenth century movement of Friedrich Ludwig Jahn, a pre-eminence absent in the Anglo-Saxon world. Nevertheless, a definite general pattern in the evolution of sport can be traced across national boundaries in Europe and North America from the late eighteenth century until the present. I want, in a capsule way, to highlight this pattern under the following rubrics:

(a) The extirpation of folk sports and games in the period of the industrial revolution

As Henri Lefebvre notes in his book, *Everyday Life in the Modern World*, everywhere in Europe, at different rhythms of pace, the medieval and peasant festivals became displaced, eclipsed and suppressed.[9] In England and the United States, this suppression of popular sport is tied to a religious motif and movement—the Puritan disdain for games. Thus in 1647 the Massachusetts Bay Company passed laws against the playing of shuffleboard and in 1650 enacted laws suppressing lawn bowling. This suppression of popular games and sport and popular festivals as locales for sport served to mobilise the peasants to work in new ways, according to a new economy of space and time. The industrial revolution taught entrepreneurs that they could no longer tolerate the inefficiency of popular festivals. The popular games connected with festivals were suppressed and, at best, went underground, roughly in the period between 1640 and 1820.

(b) The sports of the aristocracy and 'gentlemen' continued and expanded

Typically, these sports included hunting (with hounds and on horseback), horse-racing, tennis, cricket. At the beginning of the nineteenth century, the first organised sport in America was horse-racing, intended for the rich. During the nineteenth century many new games (*e.g.* soccer, baseball, later in the century, basketball) were invented. The first 'organised' games in England took place in 1849, in the United States in 1845.

(c) Around 1850 sport began to flourish in British and American schools

A frequent motif for the support of the introduction of organised sport into the schools connected sport with war, the precursor of the later slogan that Britain's war victories were prepared earlier on the playing fields of Eton. It has been said of this period of Dr. Arnold's Rugby that 'Most of the games that are now played across the world . . . were invented by a few hundred wealthy young Victorian Englishmen.'[10] The first athletic ideals for the schools emphasised aristocratic values, since almost all of the schools in the 1850s and 1860s were for aristocrats. Thus, in his inaugural address as president of Harvard College on 19 October 1869, President Charles William Eliot called for the education of 'the aristocracy which excels in manly sports, carries off the honors and prizes of the learned professions, and bears itself with distinction in all fields of intellectual labor and combat; the aristocracy which in peace stand for the public honor and renown, and in war rides first into the murderous thicket.'[11]

(d) Sports, first organised for the upper classes and in their schools, later became disseminated into the working classes beginning in the period 1860–1880

A new ideology of athleticism became dominant, whose main themes were that popular sports were class conciliatory, promoted the martial qualities and patriotism, and prevented effeminacy. Upper class sports (soccer, cricket) were exported to the lower class. This export to the working classes involved an attempt to control the working-class pubs and to remake the working class into a more malleable part of the work force, to stamp the working class with ideals of middle-class 'respectability' and 'responsibility'. John Hargreaves sums up these reasons. The twin objectives of a working-class sport movement sponsored from above were 'class conciliation and disciplining the lower orders into conformity with bourgeois norms of respectability'.[12]

Much of this outreach to the working class took place through the churches. At one time in the 1870s the overwhelming majority of soccer clubs in England were sponsored by the churches. Sports clubs, the boy scout movement (which included a vigorous culture of athleticism), the YMCA—all played a role. Historians now speak of a 'muscular Christianity', allied to this new ideology of sport which included notions of British imperialism, anti-urban, open-air naturalism and crude anti-socialist social Darwinism. In France and the United States similar forms of an ideology of athleticism emerged. Protestant 'muscular Christianity' in England and the United States had Catholic counterparts in Catholic working-class and youth sport movements in the Netherlands, Germany and Belgium at the end of the century and the beginning of the twentieth century. One can see in this phase of the development of sport for re-making and remoulding the working classes some substantiation of Michel Foucault's claim that the nineteenth century represents the century of a preoccupation by the elites of society to *discipliner et surveiller*—to discipline, channel and oversee.

(e) Naturally, the rigid control of the working-class sports organisations by the hegemonic class could not always succeed

Workers used their own sports organisations, even if sponsored from above, for their own purposes. But by the turn of the century, in most of the industrialised world, we see the rise of sport commissions and regulatory agencies. Through them, the arbiters of sport in the nation, the amateur-gentlemen, retained their earlier hegemony. Moreover, organised sports, even for the working classes, needed money and patrons. Commercial sponsors and business patrons began to subsidise the working-class sports teams. While this form of business patronage benefited the working-class sports enthusiasts, generally it excluded them from any direct decision-making about the conduct of sport.

(f) In this century, in Europe, there arose for a time an autonomous working-class sport organisation and culture sponsored by socialist groups

They organised in 1913, in Ghent, The Socialist International of Physical Education. Later, this group yielded to the new Socialist Workers Sports International (SWSI) founded in 1925. In its heyday the SWSI included 1.3

million members of whom the majority, 800,000, were members of the German *Arbeiter Turner und Sportsbund*. The SWSI organised alternative workers' olympiads in 1925 and 1931. But at any given time, more working-class athletes competed for bourgeois sponsored sports teams than for the socialist sports groups. One sports sociologist-historian blames the anti-ludic seriousness of the socialist movements for their failures in organising workers' sports. The organisers were more intent on lecturing about socialism than allowing the simple play of soccer to take place. In this respect, the churches were much more successful in organised sports during this period.

(g) The 1920s and 1930s represent a watershed period for modern sports

A dramatic increase in the size of crowds and number of spectators at sports events, the rise of the media in relation to sport (first film, then radio, later television), the increase in technological innovations (*e.g.* electric starters for horse-racing; precise underwater cameras to photo-finish a swimming meet; travel improvements which led to inter-city and inter-national sports competitions), commercialisation (paid players, spectators paying to watch professional sports, business sponsorship of prizes for athletic events), all accelerated in the 1920s and 1930s and changed the nature of an earlier, more innocent, sport. The media tended to focus on 'stars'. Technology became linked to sports both symbolically and in reality. The Italian futurists of this period saw in sport 'record-breaking' a token of technological progress. Most of the modern themes of sport: professionalisation, the sports star as hero, commercialisation, mass spectatorship and bureaucratic organisation of sport at a national and, even, international level, the fusion of sport and nationalism, can be seen to have emerged by the end of the 1930s. Martin Heidegger could lament that 'a boxer (*e.g.* Max Schmeling) is regarded as a nation's great man!'[13]

(h) With the entrance of the Soviet bloc into the International Olympic Committee in 1952 sport became a pawn of the international cold-war

(i) A critical attempt to retrieve the sports ideal from commercialisation, professionalisation and an exaggerated 'star'-based individualism occurs, starting with the late 1960s

Frequently, sports champions, themselves, have spearheaded and led this movement.[14] Since the late 1960s, the sociology of sport has proliferated. This new movement to retrieve sport looks to 'sport for all' and an understanding of sport as embodying profound human aspirations toward beauty, graceful bodies and the perfection of human achievement in bodily skills, healthy team spirit which incarnates both the agonistic impulse in humans and the ideal of local, national and international co-operation across human divisions. Feminist critics look increasingly also to sports. Sports for the elderly and the handicapped are championed as part of the sports for all movement.

3. Sport and ideology

Basically, three important divergent ideologies of sport compete for hegemony in the sports world: (1) a conservative, even, at times, fascist ideology; (2) socialist ideologies; (3) the bourgeois liberal sports ideal, a descendant of the amateur-gentleman code of chivalric honour in sports.

Already at the turn of the century, sport metaphors were widely used to justify imperialism. Colonisation was seen as a species of big-game hunting and jingoism as a form of spectator sport in the imperialistic adventure.[15] Moreover, from the nineteenth century on, the athletic ideal was closely linked to the art of war following the equations: athletes = potential soldiers and soldiers = athletes. Already in the 1830s Friedrich Ludwig Jahn's pan-German gymnastic movement drew ideological support from the motive that the gymnastics movement would prepare the bodies of German youth to wage war against Napoleon. There exist few more pathetic images than the sight of British troops, advancing over no-man's land in World War I to attack the enemy trenches, kicking a football ahead of them as they 'played on' to their deaths.

Conservatives, reactionaries and fascists frequently appeal to an image of 'sportive manhood' (exclusively masculine!) and picture both the nation's leadership and its people in athletic terms. Thus, in *Mein Kampf* Adolf Hitler saw great men as 'the marathon runners of history'. Benito Mussolini ostentatiously posed for foreign journalists while fencing, playing tennis or riding on horseback and told them he hoped that they would report how fit and expert he was.

In France, the reactionary Henry de Montherlant (as later in Japan Yukio Mishima also would do) exalted, through athletics, *la dureté*, the cult of hardness. Propaganda for Oswald Mosley, head of the British Union of Fascists during the 1930s, stressed his sport prowess. Fascists exalted the sportive, agonistic state. John Hoberman comments on differences between the political left and right in their typical resort to athletic imagery:

The left and right entertain conceptions of leadership which differ on the propriety of charismatic appeals and narcissistic self-display, hold diametrically opposite views on the use of racialistic ideas, different views on the propriety of appealing to the irrational affinities of the populace and divergent conceptions of the state as community.[16]

For the right, especially the Fascist right, notions of dynamic virility, narcissistic self-display of the leader and the party, a cult of hardness among the cadre of leadership, naked appeals to non-rational, nationalistic or racial themes underscore a latent theme of dynamic virility with the perfected body as a symbol of force. Sport is fused with theatre to produce nationalistic exaltation.

Socialist regimes notably downplay elements of narcissism and individualistic display. Thus, East German soccer teams have claimed that their style of play is 'collectivistic' and discourages the cult of the star performer. In a notable way, the leadership of eastern bloc regimes downplay explicit athletic imagery for their leadership. Rarely are Soviet leaders shown hunting, golfing, playing tennis or other sport.

The socialist ideal presents itself as more rational, hygienic, linking sport to the rational work ideal. It is premised on a man-machine symbiosis using the most advanced of sports medicine where East Germany leads the world. In 1970 Le Monde offered these impressions of an East German handball team visiting France. The writer notes 'this feeling of tranquil power, of imperturbable calm which is exuded by a team whose machinery seems tuned to perfection. Rarely has the comparison of a team to a machine been more appropriate: a steam roller. The GDR team seems to be composed of tireless human robots who can maintain the same rhythm for an hour; they are cast physically and mentally from the same mould: iron morale, nerves of steel, muscles of brass. It is almost as though one were talking about a team that was virtually metallurgical in nature.'[17]

In many ways socialist regimes and thinkers find it difficult in theory to penetrate the non-rational element of the body, the ludic as embodying a surplus charge of transcendent aspiration. Yet, in practice, despite theoretical disdain for capitalist sport's emphasis on competition, neither Soviet nor East German sport fully escape the sensationalism they decry in Western sport.

The third ideology derives from the aristocratic-gentleman's sport ideal of the nineteenth century. At its best, however, this bourgeois liberal sport envisions a class-transcending notion of 'fair play', respect for human excellence and a meritocratic ideal of competition. Most of those who seek to retrieve a new sports ideal basically seek to reform and reformulate this bourgeois ideal. In his famous essay on the Tour de France, Roland Barthes notes that—despite all the contradictions of liberal bourgeois societies reflected, pathologically, in the organisation of modern sports, 'this does not keep the *Tour* from being a fascinating national phenomenon insofar as the epic expresses that fragile moment in history in which the human person, however clumsy and deceived, nevertheless contemplates, through his impure fables, a perfect adequation between himself, the community and the universe'.[18]

4. Societal discourse models for sport

Over the years a variety of ideological and socially given models for talking about sports have been available in the West: (1) an ambivalent liberalism which links sport to rational planning; (2) a radical disillusion which despairs of the ability of modern sport to escape the corruption of civilisation. Typical of this stance is the remark of Lewis Mumford. 'Sport, which began, originally, perhaps, as a spontaneous reaction against the machine has become one of the mass-duties of the machine age';[19] (3) an aristocratic vitalism which sees a sportive style of life as re-vitalizing culture; and (4) a 'Christian fatalism' (a term applied to the position of the poet T. S. Eliot) which looks to the ideal of self-discipline in sport to provide the ascetic principle which would stop the decline of Western civilisation.[20]

But the most prevalent forms of societal discourse about sport in modern times in the West have been two: (1) the rational-recreation middle-class ideal of athleticism and fitness and (2) a discourse which assimilates sport to the discourse of commodity consumerism where sport is consumed by spectators, sold as a product, etc. Both of these prevalent discourses pervert the emancipatory ideal of sport.

5. Sport and religion

The connections between sport and religion run long and deep. Sport originated in religious festivals. The original Olympic games were banned in 351 in the name of Christian ascetical ideals against nude body exhibitionism. The Olympic games were revived in 1896 around a peculiarly modern religious ideal of chivalric internationalism. Puritans showed hostility to sports in both England and America. As we have seen, a sort of muscular Christianity, linked with the athleticism of Victorian England and on the continent, contributed to the rise of organised sports in the nineteenth century. That same muscular Christianity shows us its face again in the Fellowship of Christian Athletes and Athletes in Action (in the USA), both organs of evangelical fundamentalist Christianity. Some of that muscular Christianity appears on sport programming for the *Evangelische Omroep* network on Dutch television. Frequently, sports spectacles are called, today, new liturgies, replacing Christian liturgies as a bond of community. But it is especially the important struggle in our times to rescue the original athletic ideals from ideological distortion which calls—in the name of a renewed Christian humanism—for a new athletic ideal of *mens sana in corpore sano*. Christianity can never be indifferent to the discourses and practices of sport inasmuch as they distort the emancipatory human ideal. For the glory of God—as the Fathers of the Church remind us—is the human person come fully alive!

Notes

1. Robert J. Higgs, *Sports: A Reference Guide* (London 1982), p. 6.
2. John Hargreaves, *Sport, Power and Culture* (New York 1986), p. 5.
3. John Hoberman, *Sport and Political Ideology* (Austin, Texas 1984), p. 20.
4. Jose Ortega y Gasset, 'The Sportive Origin of the State', in *History as a System* (New York 1961), p. 17.
5. N. Ignatiev and G. Ossijsov, 'Le Communisme et le probleme des loisirs', *Esprit* (June 1959), 1061.
6. J. H. Huizinga, *Homo Ludens* (Boston 1955).
7. J. H. Huizinga, *In the Shadow of Tomorrow* (New York 1936)' p. 170.
8. Theodore Adorno, *Prisms* (London 1967), p. 81.
9. Henri Lefebvre, *Everyday Life in the Modern World* (New York 1971).
10. Philip Goodhard and Christopher Chataway, *War Without Weapons* (London 1968), p. 22.
11. Charles Eliot, *A Turning Point in Higher Education* (Cambridge, Mass 1969), p. 17.
12. Hargreaves, p. 59.
13. Martin Heidegger, *An Introduction to Metaphysics* (New York 1961), p. 31.
14. Such as Bruce Kidd and Hans Lenk who appear in this volume, each of them former athletes of distinction, each new theorists of a retrieval of the human emancipatory interest in sport.
15. *cf.* J. A. Hobson, *Imperialism: A Study* (Ann Arbor, Michigan 1972).
16. Hoberman, pp. 53–54.
17. Cited in Hoberman, p. 211.
18. Roland Barthes, *The Eiffel Tower and Other Stories* (New York 1979), p. 87.
19. Lewis Mumford, *Technics and Civilization* (New York 1963), p. 303.
20. T. S. Eliot, *The Idea of a Christian Society* (New York: 1940), pp. 12, 21–22.

Gunter Pilz

Social Factors Influencing Sport and Violence: On the 'Problem' of Football Fans in West Germany

WEEK BY week up to 150,000 mainly youthful football fans are on the move, to support their team, their club, to admire their idols, but also to experience something in the security of a like-minded group: tensions and release, a sense of community, recognition and self-affirmation, affection and emotional warmth. The background is support for a team, often unconditional, passionate expressions of joy and happiness, but also of pain and suffering. Heavy investments of time and money are accepted in order not to miss the adventure of a 'football weekend'. Of all this, however, the public see only a small—the most marketable—part: rampaging hordes of drunken fans striking terror into society; participants and others alike, with threatening gestures, extreme right-wing slogans and fights threaten public order, city centres, spectators, players officials and referees. But another side of the ceremonies, the colourful, noisy happenings of football-fan culture consist of war-songs and war cries of varying degrees of wit, fascinating outfits ('fan gear', home-produced with immense love, spirit and humour), monster flags, confetti showers, toy trumpets, drums, scarves, caps, rockets, sparklers, etc. Fan culture is full of fascinating diversity and colour. Despite this, the following article will focus only on the violent behaviour patterns in fan culture. The reason is that the exaggeration of these forms of behaviour in the media, through the exclusion of the causes and influences behind unusual behaviour by fans, and the public reaction to this, which is to call for an increase in disciplinary measures to restore order, a crackdown on the fan scene, threatens to crush it. This would deprive many young people of a youth culture which is of enormous importance in helping them to discover their identity and develop their personalities, and paradoxically escalate violent conflicts between young football fans. In other words, this article is an attempt, within the space available, to indicate the social causes and influences underlying what appears to be unusual fan behaviour in order to plead for a degree of understanding for football-fan culture and to counter hasty condemnations and criminalisation of the behaviour of young fans.[1]

1. The everyday lives of young football fans

Like all human behaviour, the violent behaviour of football fans can be properly assessed, and appropriate responses devised, only if it is placed in the context of broader social problems.

Youth is the phase of life in which young people have to construct a psycho-social identity, in which they have to prepare themselves for the adult roles of employment, starting a family, bringing up children, and citizenship, roles which they have to take on in their own way so as to fulfil themselves as personalities with particular interests and abilities. This establishing of personal identity, which has to be achieved in youth, is more difficult today. Some of the reasons can be identified, following Hornstein (1985), in the contradictions which bear upon the situation of young people today. Among the most noteworthy are the following:

(a) A prolongation of youth by the postponement of employment (*i.e.* a prolongation of economic dependence) contrasts with its curtailment by political regulations which declare young people adult at an early age and so make them responsible for their actions.

(b) There is a contradiction between the prolongation of the youth phase and the loss of significance of education and the traditional components of youth as a result of increasing unemployment and a declining number of jobs.

(c) There is a contradiction between the curtailment of the youth phase with the apparent conferral of responsibility and the simultaneous political denial to young people of the ability to take an active part in shaping society. Instead young people are relegated to a waiting state. They are superfluous and excluded from the shared responsibility they were promised.[2]

These contradictions are made more acute by the damaging effects of other social factors which are part of the setting of young people's everyday lives:

—The quest for social and personal success at all costs makes satisfactory companionship difficult.

—Alienated and meaningless working conditions create a high level of emotional stress in young people.

—Living spaces which restrict movement and offer meagre opportunities for experience and contact, together with unattractive (or no) leisure possibilities result in hanging around and killing time, and heighten the need for 'action', tension and adventure.

—A crisis in moral values, and the social impoverishment resulting from the loss of many family and neighbourhood ties essential to emotional and social stability, the 'individualisation of life-settings and life-paths' (Beck 1986), and the increased tolerance of violence lead to a loss of direction.

Moreover, some young people are in environments in which the stress on criteria of masculinity and manliness and the acceptance of physical force as a means of getting one's own way produce, encourage and require particularly unusual and aggressive forms of behaviour.

These social problem areas, merely listed here, require, for an assessment of their effect on unusual behaviour among young people, a more detailed description.

2. Unemployment and the crisis of meaning among young people

In the discussion on the significance of youth unemployment it is constantly forgotten that its damaging effects are not limited to the fact that many young people do not get a college place or a job, but include at least two others which considerably constrain the behaviour, lives and everyday surroundings of young people: (a) the scarcity of educational opportunities and jobs intensifies the problem of the quest for social and personal success at any price; and (b) a free choice of career corresponding to one's own wishes and needs is severely restricted, intensifying the problem of alienated and meaningless jobs.

In other words, the crisis of meaning as a cause of the bizarre behaviour into which many young people are locked is also a product of the crisis in the labour market. At the same time the contradictions inherent in the situation of today's young people and the background social factors intensify this crisis of meaning, substantially increasing their readiness to look for new sources of meaning.

3. The demand and quest for adventure and tension triggers off fan behaviour in young people

Another element in the picture has to do with the steadily worsening problem of the lack of experience, adventure and tension in everyday life, which is a feature of our civilisation and society. Elias (1977) has offered impressive evidence to show that, as civilisation had developed, people have been increasingly subject to a civilising pressure constantly to hold themselves and their behaviour in check, to hold back and suppress their emotions, to maintain a constant control on their urges and emotions. This inevitably has consequences, all the more since tension and affectivity are basic triggers of human action (see, for example, Csikszentmihalyi 1985). This holding in check of the system of urges and emotions creates a corresponding need for affective experiences, which, however, it is harder and harder really to satisfy in civilised industrial societies. The spaces for testing out and enjoying strong experiences are becoming steadily rarer and smaller. Elias (1978, p. 35) remarks on this:

> Today we have to hold the balance between emotional reserve, imposed on us primarily by work, and the spheres in which moderate affectivity can be satisfied. This is possible, for example, when we watch a western, go to a football match or go to a concert and let ourselves be excited by Beethoven's music.

The fact that the contents of films over the last fifty years have steadily increased in emotional charge (Kuebler 1984), that there is a strong trend to leisure activities with a marked adventure or experiential dimension (*cf.* Rittner and Mrazek 1986), is in this context evidence for an increased and increasingly unsatisfied need among people for emotion, adventure and experiences of tension. Children and young people in particular seem to resent the fact that their lives, surroundings and homes give them little or no opportunity 'to interpret or shape their surroundings in accordance with their own fantasies, projects and plans' (Becker and Schirp 1986).[3]

This lack of direct intense experiences 'leaves behind "an unsatisfied need for drama" (Mitscherlich) which seeks unrestricted outlets' (Ziegenspeck 1984, p. 101). This was expressed vividly by one football fan:

> You have to keep your mouth shut all week. Not a peep at home, at work your ideas aren't wanted. That's why we really let go at weekends. For us football is war—the team can lose if they want; we'll smash everyone.

The fan's straightforward description exactly captures the problem of holding the balance between 'imposed emotional reserve' and satisfying 'moderate affectivity'. The football weekend, against the background of the fan's everyday life, can be seen as 'adventure holidays' for the socially disadvantaged, the less financially privileged, whether in the form of active participation or enjoyment through consumption of the spectacle. A complicating factor here is the social taboo on physical violence, which increasingly gives young people fewer opportunities for letting off steam; they are ever more tightly restricted by social controls, notably by the police, and to some extent—provocative as this may sound, there is considerable evidence for it in the case of football fans—[4] treated as criminals.

Once we add to the equation these structural factors in young people's behaviour, we have to see the often irritating violent behaviour of football fans as completely appropriate responses to the contradictions of their situation (*cf.* also Bruder *et al.* 1988; Hornstein 1985), as rational actions emerging from their experiences of socialisation, the process of socialisation, and the various contexts of interaction (Heitmeyer and Peter 1988). Becker and Schirp (1986) have drawn attention to a further very important aspect which we too easily lose sight of in our excitement about the violence of young fans. Forms of 'deviant conflict resolution' are not limited to young people in a particular subculture or social stratum, but are found generally, and among adults. It is merely that other population groups possess greater financial and symbolic resources, which enable them to conceal deviations more successfully (*cf.* also Rotter and Steinert 1981). In their case violence or bizarre behaviour takes place with the public excluded, in the security of the private sphere.

4. Changes in social ties as a cause of the acceptance and legitimation of violence

The last example has to do with the class-specific differences in the way violence is held in check, with the fact that some of the young people whose behaviour provokes concern come from backgrounds in which the use of physical force is still, or once again, regarded as a legitimate means of getting one's way, of keeping or securing social prestige, as a sign of masculinity. Dunning (1983) has pointed out in this connection that, no doubt as a result of the long period of mass unemployment and the associated 'new poverty' in Great Britain, there are developing, in the social groups most affected by these problems, stronger forms of sectional binding and norms of masculinity and manliness prevalent in early phases of the development of civilisation in England. Dunning uses football hooligans to illustrate his contention of a counter-trend in civilisation to restraint of physical violence. The social groups and environments from which the majority of violent hooligans are drawn share the following characteristics:

—varying degrees of acute poverty;
—employment in simple (unskilled) and/or casual jobs, combined with a high liability to unemployment;
—a low level of formal education;
—little geographical mobility;
—mother-centred families and extensive networks of relationship;
—clear division between the sexes in activities and roles in marriage; dominance of the man;
—little supervision of children by adults;
—relatively little ability to exercise self-control and defer rewards;
—relatively poorly developed pain thresholds for physical violence;
—formation of street gangs, strong identification with close-knit we-groups combined with great hostility to outside groups.

The characteristics of these social groups listed here tend also to be mutually reinforcing, with the consequence that 'aggressive masculinity' becomes the highest value. The norms of aggressive masculinity and the relatively poorly developed capacity for self-control lead to a situation in which conflicts are usually settled directly, openly and physically. This means that fighting within and between these groups is in fact an essential means of acquiring and maintaining status in terms of the standards of aggressive masculinity. Heitmeyer and Peter (1988, pp. 47f.) point in this context to an additional problem. Norms of masculinity have become free-floating in a situation in which social inequalities have remained unchanged (or have even worsened as a result of the 'new poverty'), while class consciousness has largely broken down in the prevalent ethos of individual advancement. As a result they are less subject to mechanisms of social control with the danger that they 'can acquire a political charge and mobilising potential in the service of quite other aims and ideas'. This danger is illustrated very clearly in the chauvinistic slogans and actions of some of these young people. Violence also provides many members of these groups with a 'high'. Asked why they keep on getting involved in fights, one hooligan answered simply: 'Because it's fun.'

The currently observable escalation of violence, due in part to the repressive measures of the authorities responsible for maintaining public order and of the football authorities and the clubs, has also shifted the focus to the West German hooligan and football fan scene. 'Hooligans without weapons' is the new slogan, an appeal for fair confrontations:

There's nothing wrong with a fair fist-fight, but when it gets to baseball bats and knives it stops being funny. 'Hooligans without weapons' should be the slogan—good fighters don't need them. Only four years ago the rule was first football and then getting the team going and only then a fair scrap! When a hundred blokes in club colours . . . go yelling through the streets for a bit of aggro with some others, it's wicked!

So wrote a fan in *Fann-Treff*, a West German monthly magazine for football fans. It is of course no accident that young people choose football and its environment to supply their need for violence. As a sport, football itself embodies values and norms of masculinity and violence. Violence in the stands is easily matched by violence on the pitch (*cf.* Pilz 1989, Pilz and Wewer 1987). The intrinsic oppositional character of football means that the sport itself contributes to group identification and to the reinforcement of group solidarity in opposition to a series of easily identifiable outside groups, the opposing team and its fans (Dunning 1983).

5. Fan behaviour and fan culture: young people's cries for help and survival strategies

From what has already been said, the violent behaviour of young people which attracts public attention, in addition to being a normal form of display, must also be taken seriously as often a cry for help to society to provide meaning and a future. It is a strategy for survival, a way of getting by in a society which provides scarcely any scope for self-affirmation. It is a plea for more humane surroundings, in which emotional warmth replaces coldness, affection rejection, where tolerance, sympathy, understanding and possibilities for self-fulfilment are the norm, where there are opportunities for experiencing tensions, adventure, affectivity in general (*cf.* also Schulz 1986). These are all values and attitudes which young people look for, and for the most part find, as fans and in the many other heavily criticised youth cultures and subcultures.

This is the source of the fascination exerted by the ties of youth cultures and subcultures, but also the reason for the dangers associated with an increasing destruction and occupation ('colonisation') of these youth cultures by society and law-and-order policy. Keim (1981, p. 73) puts it clearly: Young people's bizarre or violent behaviour is a pointer to underlying inequalities, forms of coercion and exaggerated discipline, and its 'positive function' as information must be decoded, taken seriously and, where possible translated into action by (local) authorities, before there is a rush to treat this behaviour exclusively as a law-and-order problem and in the process even greater problems are created. Thirty-seven per cent of the fans questioned by Heitmeyer and Peter (1988) thought that 'people only take any notice of us if we make a bloody big noise'.

In this context another important element is that the increasing elimination of religion in our society drives many young people increasingly to 'substitute religions', 'youth religions', sects, supernatural practices and cults. It is therefore not surprising that some of the activities of football fans show religious behaviour patterns in disguised form (*cf.* Becker and Pilz 1988). Badges and banners with slogans like 'Hanover 96 is a religion. Biskup [the trainer] is our God,' or 'God with us, us against all' also point in this direction, as do the cult of stars, the deeply credulous reverence that fans show for some players or the prayer rituals fans always go through on the pitch before or after important matches. Football-fan culture must therefore be seen as another 'substitute religion' for some young people and as a receptacle for the crisis of meaning which affects young people. The importance of experiences of warmth, recognition, affection, understanding and opportunities for self-fulfilment cannot be taken too seriously as means of restricting or avoiding violence. Our attention, in other words, must be directed at young people's everyday experiences of violence (*cf.* Theunert 1987; Schibilsky 1978), and not so much at the violence they generate themselves, except in so far as we treat the latter as a pointer to inadequacies in family, school, work and society, as a cry for help and a survival strategy. This article has given no more than a fragmentary account of the rapidly increasing violence experienced by young people in our society, which should indeed make us ask why there is not much more violence by and among young people. The process of civilisation clearly bears its own fruits, but recognising this should not leave us complacent in view of the amount of violence to which young people in our society are exposed. As Elias (1981, pp. 121f.), says:

It is indeed not difficult to see that this elimination of meaning for a not inconsiderable section of the younger generation, whether by laws, unemployment or whatever, provides a wide recruiting field, not just for today's drug dealers, but also for future urban guerrillas and for future radical movements in general, whether of right or left. No-one knows what is in store for West Germany once these seeds grow.

Elias' warning, expressed in 1981, has lost none of its importance and dramatic character; on the contrary, as young people's problems have increased, his words take on even greater meaning. All that remains is the question of prevention.

6. Not smashing, but preserving and protecting: football fan culture as an opportunity for young people to discover an identity and develop their personality

Repressive, law-and-order measures do not solve the problem of violent action on the part of young football fans, as previous experience has shown. Commenting on possible preventive measures, the former chair of the advisory group set up by the minister of justice for Lower Saxony came to this remarkable and very courageous conclusion:[5]

Hasty answers should make us suspicious. Different causes call for different remedies. If the problem is individual criminality, then we need more control, more laws. However, if violence is a response to the effects of social structures, the expression of a crisis of meaning, a sign of a search for identity and a loss of perspectives, the impoverishment of familial and social ties, then the answer to the question of prevention is much more complicated, and the question of guilt involves many people, and at a very early stage. Prevention cannot be achieved by prohibitions, but under certain conditions could be achieved by retaining the provocation within the tightly confined and controlled area of the football ground.

Exclusion and isolation of football fans with violent tendencies merely drives them all the more quickly to the fringes of society and into crime. So Göbbel (1985) rightly argues: 'We must be ready to communicate, make contact with these young people and recognise the signals they are sending by their aggressive behaviour, and not be frightened off.' According, what is required are not repressive, law-and-order measures, but the provision of socio-educational and cultural facilities for young people such as the fan projects West Germany are trying to set up,[6] instead of isolation and exclusion and attempt to integrate difficult young people. Heye (1987), rightly in my view, has stressed that while youth work cannot remove the contradictions and causes of specific problems in socialisation, it does have the potential to help young people to cope better with life. Youth work must be understood as a 'counter-factual counter-culture',

as a culture against the division, isolation, polarisation and fragmentation of life-styles, against the loss of direction and meaning, against superficiality and the individualisation of life, as a culture with a 'profile', one which deliberately distinguishes itself from the leisure industry and commercialisation, which cannot be consumed like a convenience food or a tonic, but creates a stimulating environment which encourages people to discover meaning.[7]

A heavy responsibility in this area falls on the football clubs, which have tended to be obsessed with competitive sport and business and neglect their important duty to provide young people, not only with a context for competition, but also one for leisure sport and above all one which has a social and cultural dimension. In return for the fans' passionate commitment to the clubs, the clubs have given very little back. Today there is an even more urgent need for the clubs to respond, not only to the fans' needs for intimacy, but also for alternative sport and leisure facilities. Cultural work with young people in a sports club is an important contribution to controlling violence and tendencies to violence in young football fans.

There must also be an attempt to preserve and stabilise football-fan culture, since it is no less than a 'counter-factual counter-culture', a young people's answer to 'division, isolation, polarisation, the fragmentation of life-styles, the loss of direction and meaning, superficiality and individualisation'. As long as social conditions for young people do not change, these cultural expressions of young people's social interaction will be important institutions for the discovery of identity and the development of personality. As long as this situation continues, these youth cultures must also be protected against destruction or occupation by law-and-order measures. We can put it more provocatively: As long as there are no real changes at the structural level, the possibilities for reducing violence are limited. While this is the case, society must show tolerance for these violent forms of young people's search for identity (*cf.* Bruder *et al.* 1988, p. 43)

Translated by Francis McDonagh

1. On the causes specific to sport and the media, see Becker and Pilz 1988, Pilz 1989.
2. *Cf.* Baacke and Heitmeyer 1985; Bruder *et al.* 1988, pp. 13f.; Heitmeyer and Peter 1988.
3. Among the writers who have commented on this are Baacke (1979), Vaskovics (1982), and more recently especially Beck (1986), Harms, Preissing and Richtermeier (1985), Wenzel (1986) and Becker and Schirp (1986).
4. See Becker and Pilz 1988, Heitmeyer and Peter 1988, Pilz 1988.
5. Steinhilper, 'Planning and Research. Social Services' (1987).
6. On this see Bruder *et al.* 1988; Becker and Pilz 1988; Pilz 1989.
7. Heye 1987, p. 77.

Bibliography

Baacke, D. *Die 13–18jährigen* (Munich 1979).
Baacke, D., and Heitmeyer, W., eds., *Neue Widersprüche* (Weinheim and Munich 1985).
Beck, U., 'Die Zivilisation des Risikos', *Psychologie heute* (1986)11, 34–37.
Idem, *Risikogesellschaft* (Frankfurt 1986).
Becker, P., and Pilz, G. A., *Die Welt der Fans* (Munich 1988).
Becker, P., and Schirp, H., *Bewegungs- und sportorientierte Sozialarbeit mit Jugendlichen* (Marburg 1986).
Bruder, K. J., Göbbel, N., Hahn, E., Löffelholz, M., and Pilz, G. A., 'Fankultur und Fanverhalten, in Hahn, E., Pilz, G. A., Stollenwerk, H. J., and Weis, K., eds., *Fanverhalten, Massenmedien und Gewalt im Sport* (Schorndorf 1988) 11–52.
Csikzentmihalyi, M., *Das flow-Erlebnis* (Stuttgart 1985).
Dunning, E., 'Social Bonding and Violence in Sport: A Theoretical-Empirical Analysis', in Goldstein, J. H., ed., *Sports Violence* (New York 1983), pp. 129–146.
Elias, N., *Ueber den Prozeß der Zivilisation* (Frankfurt 1977).
Elias, N., 'Soziologie als Sittengeschichte', *Psychologie heute* (1978)2, 32–38.
Elias, N., 'Zivilisation und Gewalt' in Matthes, J., ed., *Lebenswelt und soziale Probleme* (Frankfurt 1981), 98–124.
Göbbel, N., *Statement at the public hearing of the Sport Committee of the West German Bundestag*, Stenographisches Protokoll Nr 33, (Bonn 1985).
Harms, G., Preissing, C., and Richtermeier, A., *Kinder und Jugendliche in der Groß stadt* (Berlin 1985).
Heye, W., 'Jugendliche zu ihrer Lebenssituation und Perspektiven für die Jugendarbeit vor dem Hintergrund sozialen Wandels', in Bezirksregierung Hannover, ed., *Fachdienst Jugendarbeit* 1, (Hanover 1987), pp. 50–91.
Hornstein, W., 'Jugend 85—Strukturwandel, neues Selbstverständnis und neue Problemlagen', *Mitteilungen der Arbeitsmarkt- und Berufsforschung* 2 (1985), 157–166.
Heitmeyer, W., and Peter, J.-I., *Jugendliche Fußballfans* (Weinheim and Munich 1988).
Keim, D., *Stadtstruktur und alltägliche Gewalt* (Frankfurt 1981).
Kübler, H.-D., 'Angstlust vor dem Bildschirm?' in Schorb, B., Schneider-Grube, S., and Theunert, H., eds., *Gewalt im Fernsehen—Gewalt des Fernsehens?* (Sindelfingen 1984), pp. 77–96.
Pilz, G. A., 'Noch mehr Gewalt ins Stadion? Zur Problematick ordnungspolitischer "Lösungen"', in Horak, R., Reiter, W., and Stocker, K., eds., *'Ein Spiel dauert länger als 90 Minuten'. Fußball und Gewalt im Europa* (Hamburg 1988), pp. 217–234.
Pilz, G. A., 'Fußballfans—ein soziales Problem?', in Klein, M., ed., *Sport und soziale Probleme* (Reinbek 1989), pp. 139–171.
Pilz, G. A., and Wewer, W., *Erfolg oder Fair Play? Sport als Spiegel der Gesellschaft* (Munich 1987).
Rittner, V., and Mrazek, J., 'Neues Glück aus dem Körper', *Psychologie heute* (1986) 11, 54–63.

Rotter, M., and Steinert, H., 'Stadtstruktur und Kriminalität', in Walter, H., ed., *Region und Sozialisation* I (Stuttgart 1981), pp. 153–185.

Schibilsky, M., 'Die verschwiegene Gewalt—Sozialpsychologische Aspekte des Gewaltproblems', *Vorgänge- Zeitschrift für Gesellschaftspolitik* 31 (1978) 1, 47–55.

Schulz, H. J., *Aggressive Handlungen von Fußballfans* (Schorndorf 1986).

Steinhilper, G., 'Kriminalpolitische Aspekte einer wirksameren Bekämpfung der Gewaltkriminalität', *Beiträge zur Inneren Sicherheit*, Schriften der Hermann-Ehlers-Akademie 21 (Kiel and Bremen 1987), 69–81.

Theunert, H., *Gewalt in den Medien—Gewalt in der Realität. Gesellschaftliche Zusammenhänge und pädagogisches Handeln* (Opladen 1987).

Vaskovics, L.-A., ed., *Raumbezogenheit sozialer Probleme* (Opladen 1982).

Wenzel, E., ed., *Die Oekologie des Körpers* (Frankfurt 1986).

Ziegenspeck, J., 'Erlebnispädagogik im Aufwind', *Sportunterricht* (1984) 3, 98–104.

Zinnecker, J., 'Straßensozialisation', *Zeitschrift für Pädagogik* 25 (1979), 727–747.

Zinnecker, J., *Jugendkultur 1940–1985* (Opladen 1987).

Nancy Shinabargar

Sexism and Sport: A Feminist Critique

THE 1980S have witnessed a rapidly changing role for women in sport. At the international level, women's participation in the Summer Olympics has nearly doubled in twelve short years, rising from 1,274 in 1976 to 2,476 in 1988. The increased participation of women in sport is being felt by many countries on the national level as well. In the United States, for example, women have risen from comprising only 15.6% of all competitive university athletes in the early 1970s to comprising over 33% in 1988, including 46% of competitive university athletes in sports with male-female divisions.[1] Not only are women competing in increasing numbers, but they are competing successfully in sports traditionally reserved for men such as cycling, kayaking, soccer, rifle and pistol, shot put, luge, rowing, javelin throw, high jump, triathlon, field hockey and ice hockey. But these very achievements of women raise serious questions: Why do the athletic achievements of women remain so invisible in society as a whole? What barriers of sexism still remain for women in contemporary society? To understand this problem this article will examine three important links between sexism and sport in contemporary society from a feminist perspective and the social cost to women that sexism in sport entails.

1. Sport and gender socialisation: the root of sexism and sport

Sport as a social institution articulates a distinctive set of social orientations or obligatory norms for cultural values and defines patterns of socially-acceptable behaviour. Harry Edwards, the première sociologist of sport in the United States, observes that sport disseminates and reinforces

44

values regulating behaviour and goal attainment and determines acceptable solutions to social life within the dominant cultural ideal.[2] Sport as a social institution plays a powerful role in the cultural definition of male and female. As Patricia J. Murphy (1988) notes, 'The social organization of sport provides, through its images, ideologies and structures a mechanism for maintaining and legitimating a particular organization of gender in society.'[3] The social organisation of gender in sport reflects and reinforces a situation of gender stratification in society. The specific cultural expectations of what constitutes 'proper' female or male behaviour is communicated through an ideology of sex roles in the process of gender socialisation.

Sport in the modern period has reinforced the sexual division of labour in society.[4] Historically, sport channelled men to the 'cultural project' while women were socialised away from sport into more traditionally 'feminine' activities. Gender stratification and an ideology of sex roles proscribed women's sport participation and rendered it problematic. In the United States, as late as the 1970s competitive women athletes experienced their sport involvement as a 'social anomaly' in the male-dominated world of sport.[5] For males, however, sport is perhaps this country's most important social rite for masculine identity. Sport sociologist Wilbert Marcellus Leonard (1980) observes that in the United States sport functions as a near-obligatory male rite-of-passage.[6] Sport by its very definition in American culture embodies idealised masculine traits of competitiveness, aggression and loyalty.[7]

The ideology of sex roles generated by gender stratification and gender socialisation made the combined role of 'women' and 'athlete' virtually impossible in the United States until the last few years, as the work of Edwards (1973) and D. Stanley Eitzen and George H. Sage (1978) found.[8] Sex barriers were not easily crossed. In 1967 Katherine Switzer became the first woman to run the Boston Marathon and was suspended by the Amateur Athletic Union for her action. The sex-testing of women at the Olympic Games and other international meets left the impression, as one American athlete said, 'You're so good, we just can't believe you're a woman. So prove it.'[9] An ideology of sex roles that depicted women primarily as care-givers and not achievers, as passive and ornamental, as lacking in purpose and direction is directly challenged by the competitive athletic woman. Woman athletes who did cross the sex barrier in sports traditionally reserved for men were often stigmatised as 'masculine' or 'unnatural'.[10]

An ideology of sex roles also creates a certain social construction of gender in which unequal rewards and opportunities for women in sport are legitimised. Professional tennis and golf, which have separate female and male divisions and are therefore comparable, will serve as an example of the lower social valuation placed on women's sport achievements. In 1978, the top five US women tennis professionals earned a combined total of $783,000; the top five US men earned a total of $2,061,000.[11]. In 1984 the top five US women golfing professionals earned a combined total of $1,129,000; the top five US male golfers earned $2,122,000. By 1988 the winnings of the top five US women golfers had risen only slightly to $1,654,000; the winnings of the top five US male golfers nearly doubled in that same four-year period to reach a total of $4,418,000.[12] The year 1988 marked a level of near-parity in the winnings for the top five US male and female tennis players.[13] But sport as a social institution continues to reinforce and reflect the lower valuation placed on women's economic activity when team sports are examined. In the United States professional team sport opportunities for women remain highly restricted and have limited economic impact. Major League Volleyball began for women in 1987, but the Women's Basketball League and the International Women's Professional Softball League lasted only a few seasons, folding in the early 1980s.[14] While women's team sports struggle for survival, a single male professional team event such as the 1988 Superbowl generates an estimated $200 million in revenue from television contracts, gate receipts and other commercial activity.

2. Female and athlete: the structural problem of sexism and sport

The dramatic increase of women in sport has challenged the dominant ideology of sex roles disseminated and reinforced by sport. The phenomenon of sexism *in* sport is one response to the perceived threat to male identity posed by women in sport. The virulent reaction which the combined role of 'woman' and 'athlete' first evoked in the United States, a country with a history of activity for women's rights dating back to the 1840s, indicates the severe challenge to female role expectations that the sport involvement of women represented. As late as 1974 the legendary football coach of Ohio State University, Woody Hayes, could voice the most derogatory comments about female athletic participations at a nearby university without facing suspension from coaching:

> I hear they're even letting w-o-m-e-n in their sports program now (referring to Oberlin College). That's your Women's Liberation boy— bunch of goddam lesbians ... You can bet your ass that if you have women around—and I've talked to psychiatrists about this—you aren't

going to be worth a damn. No sir! Man has to be dominant . . . The best way to treat a women, . . . is to knock her up and hide her shoes.[15]

In virtue of presenting herself as 'female' and 'athlete', the woman in sport questions the isomorphism between sport and male identity. By choosing a physically competitive life in university or professional athletics, women call into question the underlying cultural definitions of female and male in sport and society in a very public way. Sexism, as one response to women in sport, can generally be defined as, 'an unfavourable attitude toward and the unequal treatment of persons of one sex, based on an elaborate series of negative traits assumed to be distributed among this sex'.[16] But sexism, like racism, can also comprise a response of exclusivity and differentiation that suggests inferiority. Paul Willis (1982) notes that sexism in sport can be perceived in the 'gaps' that disclose the differentiation of women from men in sport.[17] One such gap is the exaggerated difference between female and male sport achievement. Despite the fact that female athletes can perform up to 90% to 93% of a male athlete's physical capacity in sports such as track and swimming, women are perceived as being significantly weaker. Because the 'fact' of female difference, no matter how small, cannot be denied, it becomes a tailor-made opportunity for suggesting female sports inferiority.[18]

The structural discrimination against women in sport can also appear as the male distinction between the 'women's game' and the 'real game'. As Mary A. Boutilier and Luncinda SanGiovanni (1983) observe, even when women play basketball, football or tennis, men are quick to distinguish the 'real' game they play from the less valued 'women's game' of the very same sport.[19] These attitudes toward women's sport achievements are rooted in childhood experience of play. As Roberta S. Bennett and her colleagues note, play for girls usually occurs alone or with one or two others. When girls do engage in organised athletic activities, success is attributed to 'luck'; failure is attributed to a lack of 'skill'.[20] For boys, even casual play frequently involves many players and complex rules. Success for boys is attributed to 'skill'; failure is attributed to 'back luck'.[21] The result is that girls internalise a pattern of immaturity, a lack of self-confidence and self-control over their own bodies. The diminishment and exclusion of women from male activity continues the definition and validation of male identity in contemporary society. Boutilier and SanGiovanni write:

What secures and enhances activities prescribed for men is, in large measure, due to women's exclusion from them. The absence of women and of attributes defined as feminine are two of the elements that clarify men's role. Men are what women are not; men do what women cannot.[22]

This analysis of sexism in sport suggests that the nature of sexism in the institution of sport is a structural and systemic problem. As Richard E. Lapchick, Director of the Center for the Study of Sport in Society at Northeastern University in Boston observes (1966), 'in spite of all the gains ... there is still a great void in the second half of the 1980s regarding women in the structure of sports administration and equal spending on women's athletics'.[23] Women in positions of academic leadership in the United States such as Donna A. Lopiano of the University of Texas, are calling for the accomplishment of feminist objectives in the American intercollegiate sport system as one response to the structural problem of sexism.[24] How contemporary sport can be reclaimed to function for women's benefit is the question we shall examine next.

3. Toward a feminist critique of sexism and sport

Contemporary sport feminism offers both a critique of sexism in sport as a social institution and a vision of how sport can be transformed to reflect a feminist perspective on human activities and interaction. Indirectly, the critique of sport feminism offers a vision of sport as a *human* good rather than an institution that abuses and dehumanises athletes, contracts and markets players as if they were commodities and educates the youth of many countries in a language of violence and domination. Our task in this section is twofold: (1) to articulate the contemporary sport feminist critique of sexism in sport in the United States; (2) to offer the feminist vision of the transformation of sport as a social institution.

The feminist critique of sport as a social institution offered by sport sociologists such as Boutilier and SanGiovanni, Susan Birrell, Marie Hart, Diana M. Richter, Robert S. Bennett and her San Francisco colleagues, and Mary E. Duquin suggest that the underlying problem in sport is the patriarchal structure of society and its assumptions about women's inferiority. As Duquin (1982) convincingly shows, patriarchy as a set of social practices and social relations which allow men to dominate women are identifiable in the institutional structure of sport. Five patriarchal practices that Duquin identifies are relevant to our assessment of feminist sport theory in addressing sexism in sport in the United States. They are: (1) a 'predominantly male administrative system' which results in 'economic advantages for those in power', (2) male power over women expressed through 'male aggression and dominance', and 'male bonding', (3) 'institutionalised power over women's sexuality' seen in the low priority accorded to women's health issues in educational sport institutions; (4) a 'negative stereotype of women in sport, including questions of sexual orientation', and 'homophobia', which makes female bonding difficult; (5) socialisation that limits women's sense of potential and achievement.[25] The feminist critique of sexism in sport is confirmed in part by a consideration of the recent legal and social changes in the United States regarding the historical pattern of discrimination against women in sport.

Since 1979 discrimination on the basis of sex in any programme or activity by an education institution receiving federal funding has been prohibited under federal law. Meant to correct a situation in which sport was labelled as 'the most sexually segregated of America's civilian social institutions', this legislation, known as 'Title IX', has unquestionably led to significant changes in institutional discrimination against women in sport.[26] In 1971–72 only 7% of all high school athletes in competitive sport were young women; in 1987–88 that figure was over 34%, or approximately 1.85 million young women.[27] In competitive university athletics, women comprised over 41% of all athletes in 1987–88 in programmes affiliated with the National Collegiate Athletic Association (NCAA), the largest US university sport organisation, excluding football, or approximately 90,000 athletes.[28] A close examination of individual NCAA sports reveals an even greater parity in university sports with male-female divisions for 1987–88: (1) women comprise 46% of *all* NCAA basketball players; (2) women constitute 50% of *all* NCAA swimmers; (3) women are 49% of *all* NCAA tennis players; (4) women are 44% of *all* NCAA cross country runners: (5) women comprise 47% of *all* NCAA rowing teams.[29]

The significance of this structural change in American sport is now a matter of debate among sport sociologists in the United States. There are some preliminary indications that the increased prominence and importance of women's sport has actually led to a decrease in athletic leadership positions for professional sport women. The research of Bonnie Parkhouse and Milton Holmen (1980) found that of 768 new coaching positions for Women's teams in 335 institutions between 1974 and 1979, 724 went to men.[30] Vivian Acosta and Linda Carpenter (1983) found that women's teams increased by 17% from 1977–82 but the proportion of women's teams coached by women decreased from 58.2% to 52.4%.[31] Inequitable media exposure, particularly television, also confirms in part the feminist critique of sexism in sport. In 1988–89 the largest cable sports network in the United States, ESPN, televised 213 regular-season NCAA basketball games. Only two games, or less than 1% of the total, were women's games despite the fact that women comprise 46% of all NCAA basketball players on 756 teams.[32].

For sport feminists such as Patricia J. Murphy (1988), the Title IX legislation represents an 'assimilationist' perspective on women in sport that emphasises an uncritical adaptation of women to the existing institutional structure of sport.[33] The benefits of such assimilation are dubious. In 1985 the Cheyney University women's basketball team became the first NCAA women's basketball team to be placed on probation for recruiting violations. In 1988 Kris Durham, an outstanding basketball player recruited by over 200 colleges, left the University of Tennessee while her team was ranked first in the country to play for lesser-known Seton Hill. 'Basketball had become a 24-hour job', Durham told an interviewer for the *New York Times*. 'On the court, on the track, in the weight room. The program was too intense. I didn't want to play at that level.'[34] To what extent does the assimilation of women to the male sport system of university athletics imply adaptation to the use of performance-enhancing drugs, cash payoffs to key players, recruiting violations, grade-fixing to maintain athletic eligibility and a commercialisation of sport in which the 18-year-old athlete is treated like a commodity? 'It's a business,' Durham said. 'You're like a piece of land. They'll do anything to get it, but once they get it, they'll do what they want with it.'[35]

The critique of sport feminism in the United States offers a vision of how sport can be reclaimed to function for the benefit of women, and, indirectly, how sport can be transformed into a *human* good. The sport feminist position advocated by Robert S. Bennett, K. Gail Whitaker, Nina Jo Woolley Smith and Anne Sablove of San Francisco State University argues that sport can enable women to reclaim themselves as competent, whole and self-directing persons.[36] Noting that women are socialised into non-ownership of their bodies at an early age, they suggest that sport is one way of empowering women to achieve the kind of 'movement literacy' which can overcome a learned sense of physical and social inadequacy.[37]

The reclamation of sport to function for the benefit of women has two main objectives: (1) the development of women as 'skilful performers' through sport: (2) the transformation of sport to reflect women-centred and women-directed values. As Bennett *et al.* observe, the separation of women from experiences that promote movement skills is a separation from self-possession and self-control.[38] The transformation of sport to reflect women-centred values requires that the rules of the game in contemporary sport be changed from an activity defined by dominance and submission, aggression and assault, violence and survival to reflect a new social construction of gender in sport and society. They write:

Nonetheless, it is possible to envision changing the values and the parameters of sport (and of the social system) which perpetuate dominance. They are, after all, man-made devices. One can envision changing the means by which successes are defined and measured, so that the value would be in cooperative growth and in seeking mutual joy in one another's accomplishments rather than in annihilation of an opponent. One can envision shared decision-making, shared knowledge, a return of control of sport to the performers, and their empowerment as subjects rather than their oppression as objects.[39]

4. Conclusion

The feminist critiuqe of sexism in sport reflects a new vision of the social construction of gender in which sport as a social institution can be reclaimed to function as a *human* good. In our study of sport as a social institution, we have found the problem of sexism in sport to be structural and systemic in nature, rooted in the function of sport as a highly symbolic public space in which the sexism of contemporary society is reflected and reinforced. Contemporary sport feminism in the United States argues against the uncritical assimilation of women to the male-dominated system of sport on the grounds that sport must become more women-centred, women-directed and women-affirming. Indirectly the critique of sport feminism shows the need for a *human* liberation of sport in which sport as a social institution is transformed to reflect an inclusive complementarity of gender with respects and values the feminine and masculine in sport and society. The dramatic increase of competitive, self-possessed and self-directed young women on the basketball court, on the track, in the soccer field is both a statement about women as skilfully competent persons in sport and as skilfully competent agents in society. The critique of sexism that sport feminism offers is about much more than simply changing the rules of the sport game.

Notes

1. National Collegiate Athletic Association, '1987–88 Participation Study— Women', and '1987–88 Participation Study—Men' (Mission, Kansas 1989). The sports compared include basketball, cross country, swimming, tennis, indoor and outdoor track, volleyball, golf, gymnastics and crew for Divisions I, II and III.
2. Harry Edwards, *Sociology of Sport* (Homewood, Illinois 1973), 90–91.
3. Patricia J. Murphy, 'Sport and Gender', in *A Sociological Perspective of Sport*, by Wilbert Marcellus Leonard II (New York [3]1988), p. 272.
4. B. Kidd, 'Sports and masculinity', *Queen's Quarterly* 94 (Spring 1987) 116–131.

5. Jan Felshin, 'The Triple Option ... for Women in Sport', in *Sport in the Sociocultural Process*, ed. Marie Hart and Susan Birrell (Dubuque, Iowa 1981), p. 488.
6. Wilber Marcellus Leonard, *A Sociological Perspective of Sport* (Minneapolis, Minnesota 1980), p. 191.
7. Edwards, *Sociology of Sport*, pp. 94, 103–109, 114–119.
8. D. Stanley Eitzen and George H. Sage, *Sociology of American Sport* (Dubuque, Iowa 1978), p. 261.
9. Jane Frederick, quoted in Leonard, *A Sociological Perspective of Sport* (1980), p. 195.
10. Murphy, *A Sociology of Sport* (1988), p. 273.
11. Women's International Tennis Association, Miami Beach, Florida; Association of Tennis Professionals, Ponte Vedra Beach, Florida. 1978 US women: Evert, King, Casals, Austin, Russell. 1978 US men: Dibbs, McEnroe, Connors, Gerulaitis, Solomon.
12. Ladies Professional Golf Association Tour, Sugarland, Texas; Professional Golf Association, Ponte Vedra Beach, Florida; 1984 US women; King, Sheehan, Bradley, Alcott, Inkster; 1988 US women: Turner, Sheehan, Jones, Lopez, Walker; 1984 US men: T. Watson, O'Meara, Bean, D. Watson, Kite; 1988 US men: Strange, Beck, Sindelar, Green, Kite.
13. This list does not include Martina Navratilova, who became a US citizen in 1981.
14. Murphy, *op cit.* n. 3, p. 281.
15. Woody Hayes, quoted in Eitzen and Sage, *Sociology of American Sport*, p. 275.
16. *Ibid.*, pp. 262–263.
17. Paul Willis, 'Women in Sport Ideology', in *Sport, Culture and Ideology*, ed. Jennifer Hargreaves (London 1982), p. 120.
18. *Ibid.*
19. Mary A. Boutilier and Lucinda SanGiovanni, *The Sporting Women* (Champaign, Illinois 1983), p. 103.
20. Robert S. Bennett, K. Gail Whitaker, Nina Jo Woolley Smith and Anne Sablove, 'Changing the Rules of the Game: Toward a Feminist Analysis of Sport', *Women's Studies International Forum* 10:4 (1987), 369–379.
21. *Ibid.*, p. 371.
22. Boutilier and SanGiovanni, *The Sporting Women*, p. 103.
23. Richard E. Lapchick, ed., *Fractured Focus: Sport as a Reflection of Society* (Lexington, Mass. 1986), p. 137.
24. Donna A. Lopiano, 'A Political Analysis of the Possibility of Impact Alternatives for the Accomplishment of Feminist Objectives Within American Intercollegiate Sport', in *Fractured Focus: Sport as a Reflection of Society*, ed. Richard E. Lapchick, pp. 163–165.
25. Mary E. Duquin, 'Feminism and Patriarchy in Physical Education', in *Studies in the Sociology of Sport*, ed. Aidan O. Dunleavy, Andrew W. Miracle, and C. Roger Rees (Fort Worth, Texas 1982), pp. 167, 169, 170, 171, 173.

26. Edwards, *Sociology of Sport*, p. 101.
27. National Federation of State High School Associations, Kansas City, Missouri, March 1989.
28. National Collegiate Athletic Association, '1987–88 Participation Study— Women', and '1987–88 Participation Study—Men'.
29. *Ibid.*
30. Bonnie L. Parkhouse and Milton G. Holmen, 'Multivariate Considerations in the Selection of Coaches for Female Athletes: A Demographic and Attitudinal Inquiry', unpublished paper, University of Southern California, 1980, quoted in Ann Ulhir, 'The Wolf is Our Shepherd: Shall We Not Fear?' in *Sport in Contemporary Society: An Anthology*, ed. D. Stanley Eitzen (New York ²1984), p. 378.
31. *Chronicle of Higher Education* (New York), 30 March 1983, p. 21.
32. David Nagle, ESPN, Bristol, Connecticut, March 1989.
33. Murphy, *A Sociological Perspective of Sport* (1988), p. 282.
34. Kris Durham, quoted in 'For A Star, Top 20 Has Little Heart', in *The New York Times*, 22 February 1989, B15.
35. *Ibid.*
36. Bennett *et al.* 'Changing the Rules of the Game', in *Women's Studies International Forum*, pp. 369–370.
37. *Ibid.*, p. 370.
38. *Ibid.*, pp. 370–373.
39. *Ibid.*, p. 378.

PART II

Sport and National Culture: Two Case Studies

Roberto DaMatta

Sports *in* Society: *Futebol* as National Drama

MY PURPOSE in this article is to discuss how a certain vehicle for sports, a football association (hereafter referred to as *futebol*), is also a vehicle for a series of dramatisations of Brazilian society. Instead, however, of analysing *futebol* in contrast to society as is usual in this type of inquiry[1], I will study *futebol* within society; in the belief that attaining a thorough sociological understanding of Brazilian *futebol* will improve the possibility of reaching a deeper sociological interpretation of Brazilian society itself. On the other hand, I think that this approach demonstrates how a particular social activity with universal characteristics was appropriated and adapted variously in different societies.

Inspired by the works of Victor Turner and Max Gluckman (*cf.* Turner 1957, 1974; Gluckman 1958, 1962), I will make use of the concept of 'dramatisation' but hope to add to this conceptualisation, because I consider dramatisation a basic element of the process of ritualisation (*cf.* DaMatta 1979). My understanding is that ritual cannot exist without drama and that the distinctive characteristic of dramatisation is to call attention to relationships, values or ideologies which could not otherwise be duly isolated from the routines of daily life. By studying *futebol* as drama, I intend to take these activities as special social forms through which a society lets itself be perceived by its members.

1. Futebol as opium of the people

But in order to do so, we have first to criticise the trivial notion that '*futebol* is the opium of the people', a notion well linked to the dichotomy between sports and society. Indeed, it does not take too much thinking to discover that the opposition, sports/society, is just one pair in a long list of such typical oppositions: nature/society, ritual/society, politics/society, economy/society, supernatural/natural, etc., whereby confrontation, delimitation or reduction is often postulated between the contrasting elements. On one side, we have an individualised entity: sports, nature or a social institution; while on the other, we have another individualised entity: society. The idea inherent in these oppositions is that a functional relationship exists between one term and the other. It follows that sports will *do* something *for*, *with* or *against* society, thus acting as a positive, negative or neutral instrument in relationship to the social system. With respect to *futebol* and Brazilian society, a relationship of mystification is often postulated. Soccer is held to be an opium of Brazilian society just as the economy is its 'real' base, as if *futebol* and the economy were exogenous realities which could exist apart from society. In this view, *futebol* is seen as one way of distracting the attention of Brazilian people from other problems that are taken to be more basic. If the social scientist were considering a political party or an economic activity, the same equation could be utilised, but he would be more careful about saying that a certain political party or economic institution is 'an opium of the people' simply because in our current conceptualisation of society, politics and economics are seen to be more 'serious' and basic than *futebol*. This perspective also implies that the Brazilian people are incapable of correctly perceiving their socio-historical position and understanding the relationship between *futebol* and society.

This thesis reflects a familiar 'utilitarian-functionalist' flavour so in vogue in the social sciences, as has been disparaged—among others—by Marshall Sahlins (1976, 1978). According to this utilitarian thesis, if *futebol* is an important institution, it ought to be carrying out a certain well-defined social function *in relationship* to society. In this case, its function (or 'utility') is to divert the attention of the people and to mystify them. As if the only people who know this 'real' function of *futebol* in Brazilian society are its critics and the dominant class who use *futebol* as opium for the masses. The masses themselves remain astonishingly ignorant, incapable of perceiving their systematic deception.

I think it is fundamental to present a different position. My suggestion is that we should try to understand sports *in* society. We will not try to study the opposition between two individualised and empirically reified terms, but will focus instead on interconnections and expressions of one term by the other. The basic assumption is that sports are a part of society just as much as society is also a part of sports. In fact, it is impossible to understand one without referring to the other. Sports and society are like the two sides of the same coin and not like a roof in relation to the foundations of a house. Their relationship is not one of stratification, as if sports were a later, superfluous activity that was invented *after* work, but has—like anything else—a dialectical, reflexive, link with society.

The basic issue is not to discern the functions and utility of sports in a given social system, but rather to try to discover the expression of some values of society through this 'media' called 'sports'. In doing so we do not ask about what sports *do* for society, but what is society making available to its members in the universe of sports? What relationships can we enjoy, renew and establish while involved in sports? What emotions can we feel and which sentiments must we avoid when we are experiencing a *futebol* game? What sorts of chaos and which dimensions of order do we actually come into contact with in the world of sports? What are the surroundings, rules, objects, social relations and values which sports enable us to conceive of and live out? Finally, when it manifests itself through its sportive dimension what does society itself look like?

2. The specificity of Brazilian soccer

Let us compare the relative significance of soccer in different societies by considering the way sport in general and soccer in particular are conceptualised in the British and North American systems, in contrast to the way in which the same activities are conceived in Brazil. The first difference is that, in the Anglo-Saxon world, football, tennis, baseball, soccer, golf, etc. . . . are 'sports' while for Brazilians the word *futebol* never appears alone, being always preceded by the qualifier, '*jôgo*' (game). Thus in Brazil, we say: 'a *jôgo-de-futebol* (soccer game) will take place'. One does not merely speak of *futebol* but comments on or argues about a *jôgo-de-futebol*. This is an important point because the specific position of soccer (and of sport in general) varies from society to society. As a matter of fact, the association between soccer and 'game' in the Brazilian case entails two ideas which are separate in American society. The idea of 'game of chance' which, in Brazil, is indicated by the expression *jôgo* (=*jôgo-de-azar*), in the United States and in England is expressed by 'gamble', representing something absent from sport in its strict sense (although it can clearly be a part of its constellation or the overall organisation it articulates). The other idea is directly related to the activity of sport which is, according to the standard definition of the Oxford Dictionary, 'a diversion of the nature of a contest, played according to rules and decided by superior skill, strength, or good fortune'. It should be observed that the concept of 'sport' in the Anglo-Saxon social universe stresses competition, technique and strength, with luck only coming last. One has the impression that in the United States and England the domain of sport has very much to do with body control and with the co-ordination of individuals to form a team which, in this social universe, represents a strong form of the collective. In Brazil, 'sport' is experienced much as a game. It is an activity which requires tactics, psychological determination and technical skills, but it also depends on the uncontrollable forces of fortune and destiny. It happens quite often that in Brazil, after a soccer game, commentaries refer not only to the fact that one of the teams played against the adversary, but also against 'destiny' or 'bad luck' which must be changed or corrected in order to bring about future victories.

3. Brazilian soccer versus American and European soccer

This explains why in certain countries soccer is associated with a national lottery system. In the specific case of Brazil the so-called *loteria esportiva*, a lottery system associated with soccer matches, makes it possible to refer to a set of values that are related to the Brazilian system of good and bad fortune, including magical appeals to supernatural beings of the so-called Afro-Brazilian religions (like the *orixás* of Umbanda and Candomblé), and popular saints of Brazilian Roman Catholicism. Because of the association of soccer with ideas of misfortune through the *loteria esportiva* (which pays prizes in the millions), one can speak of several soccer games which are 'played' on different levels every time that an important match happens. There is the 'empirical' or 'real' game which takes place in the soccer stadium, played by professionals. There is another game which takes place in 'real life' played by the Brazilian people in its constant search to change its destiny, a hope deeply associated with the destiny of the *'futebol* team' they support. And there is a third game played in the 'other world' where supernatural entities are summoned to exert influence on 'our team', thus promoting an eventual transformation of our social position by virtue of the victory of the team of our choice. All this illustrates how a given institution, in this case, a 'football association'—a sports organisation invented by the British, can be appropriated and used in different ways by different societies. Indeed, in this context it is worth-while mentioning the way American commentators tend to see soccer as a mild form of play projecting onto it the position it has in the overall structure of sports in the United States. But in Brazil, soccer is not a game to be played by children and woman, but is a serious activity with deep religious overtones.

All soccer fans know that Brazilian and European soccer are different because when Brazilians play soccer they reveal a great capacity to improvise. In Brazil the emphasis is on the team and also on the individuality of the players who—as a rule—have a highly developed sense of ball-control. In this way soccer becomes a source of individual expression in Brazilian society. In fact, it is through soccer that the Brazilian people especially the so-called 'Brazilian masses'—acquire a positive social and political identity. In the same way someone belonging to the unknown masses—the so-called *povão* in Brazilian Portuguese—might change into a star of a soccer team and become a super-person and the centre of attention, an outstanding personality who cannot be replaced (*cf.* DaMatta 1979). But in order to relate soccer and the Brazilian collective identity, let me take two basic dramatisations of soccer in Brazil and study their most important social and political implications.

4. Two dramatisations of soccer

(a) The question of destiny in opposition to biography

Destiny as a social category refers to the effort made by some societies to mediate between the set of impersonal forces that run the world without human interference and the individual persons with their own biographies, desires and needs who live in the world. As a social category, the idea of 'destiny' makes it possible to form a 'bridge' between the individualised biographical level and the forces in the system that are thought of as tending to 'play' with each biography and every will. I think that this confrontation is one the critical points of difference in social systems not completely characterised by individualism, such as is the case of societies which passed through the Protestant Reformation and the Industrial Revolution.

A soccer game clearly entails a complex interaction between universal rules (the rules of the game) and individual wills. The resulting victory or defeat seems to provide a good metaphor for the interplay between destiny and biography, a basic theme of Brazilian society. Thus, in *futebol*, as in so-called 'real life', men are related to each other as members of families and they expect to win and behave in a certain way. They cannot control, however, the actions of the opposing teams nor its players' ability, teamwork and errors. Even when a team seeks victory through magical means, which is very common in Brazilian *futebol*, a high probability of victory can only be hoped for but never expected with any degree of certainty. The game reveals a complex interaction between a team and its opponent, between the team and itself, between the two teams and the rules governing the spectacle, and between the teams, rules and public and the controllers of the match (the referees and linesmen). It is all these interactions that help create the fascination for soccer. It is without doubt this complexity which lets us take the game of *futebol* as a metaphor for life itself, thus expressing some of the basic conflicts in Brazilian society.

Imagine a well trained team with highly motivated, skilled players, all well disciplined and in excellent physical condition. And let us add another element to these factors: our imagined team has had a perfect season. In this team's next and crucial match—the decisive contest for winning the title of the World Soccer Championship—it will face a strong opponent whose season has been excellent, though not as consistent as the first team's and clearly inferior by all objective standards. In fact, the opponent's season has been sufficiently inconsistent so that the supreme title could only be won by a victory, since a tie would give the championship to our imagined team. In the minds of everybody, then, there is no doubt that the championship would be won by the more highly motivated, better trained team that so far had had a perfect season. This kind of thinking has become accepted as a matter of justice and social order. But let us imagine that this invincible team loses the decisive game.

Brazilian defeat in soccer

How can this happen? This was the question that everybody was asking in Brazil when, in June 1950, the Brazilian team was defeated in Rio de Janeiro by the Uruguayan team in the finals of the world soccer championship. The memory of this defeat ought to be investigated from our particular point of view. First, it has perhaps been the greatest felt tragedy experienced in contemporary Brazilian history because it involved all social segments of Brazilian society and brought unity through the recognition of the loss of such an historic opportunity. Secondly, the defeat was socially significant because it occurred at the beginning of a decade in which Brazil was seeking to make her mark as a nation with a great destiny. This resulted in a tireless search for explanations for this shameful defeat, and it has been through this process of 'allocating responsibilities' (*cf.* Gluckman 1972) that we ought to find the social background for this dramatisation.

After the defeat, *destino* (destiny, fate, lot) and *má-sorte* (bad luck) were constantly discussed, and 'destiny' indicated that this outcome was characteristic of a society which intended to escape from its traditional posture of inferiority and defeat. Such a portentous blow subjected many Brazilians to deep disillusionment about *futebol* schedules, purposes and forecasting, etc. How can all the effort have mattered, they were asking bitterly, if in the end they were defeated and luck did not smile on them? The explanations, however, did not remain this simple for long. As the work of Guedes (1977) reveals, various journalists began to examine the forces of destiny more closely and identified racial factors therein. This defeat in *futebol*, they said, was directly attributable to our unfortunate 'racial composition' and to the enormous burden we were bearing as a society made up of 'inferior groups' such as Indians and Negroes. Three Negro players from the defensive force of this select Brazilian play-off team were set aside as examples of this sad fate of a sick and inferior country.[2]

As I have already observed, there is a close relationship between *jôgo de futebol* and *jôgo da vida* (game of life) with the result that the defeat by Uruguay was like a defeat of the Brazilian national society itself, subdued as it always was by the impersonal forces of destiny. Thus, *futebol* brought to the surface a social problem which Brazilians had wanted to overcome for a long time, which is the dilemma between strong, explicit motivations and the impersonal, uncontrollable forces of a prejudiced view of history in terms of racism. Thus this defeat in *futebol* resulted in reactivating a pessimistic tradition, expressed through the dramatic representations of a society which believes itself to be racially impure. Here, roughly speaking, is the dramatic situation portrayed through soccer which resulted in the resuscitation of old racist theories which still play an important part of Brazilian ideology.

I believe we must search for the relationship between sports and society at this level of sociological abstraction, that is, when *jôgo de futebol* generates a network reflecting the whole society. Since soccer is easy to watch, it also serves to dramatise and bring the dilemmas of a society into focus. In this way, the theme of destiny, as a category expressing the conflict between individual wills and impersonal forces, appears also in the erudite racism of intellectuals for whom the fate of Brazil is, or was, advanced by impersonal forces with a biological history whose dynamics were far beyond the volition of men. On the other hand, in the *carnaval* and in popular music (as well as in popular religiosity) destiny is a basic factor in coping with suffering.

Brazilian soccer success

Within this cultural picture where destiny occupies such an important place, Brazil's winning of the Third World Soccer Championship in 1970 can be understood as an expression of *national vengeance*—a unique moment in which an entire society could, finally, experience victory against these impersonal forces which had always placed it 'in a bottomless pit'.

Simultaneously with this process of the re-evaluation of our posture in the world, came a redefinition of the value of race, especially of the blacks, as being fundamentally positive. I think we can best understand the phenomenon of Pelé, and his being crowned King of *Futebol*, from this point of view; for, if the Negro was responsible for the tragic defeat of 1950 because he was seen as being inferior by racist Brazilians, surely the super-Negro, Pelé, was now responsible for the Victory of Brazil in the subsequent world championships.[3] And this is not all, for through *futebol* another very important dramatisation closely related to the one just studied can be portrayed. This pertains to the reification of Brazil itself, which this game makes possible when an abstract entity such as a country, a nation or a people can be experienced as something visible, physical and distinct such as a team that suffers, thrills, conquers adversaries and responds to our positive and negative motivating influences. In a country where the popular masses never have a voice except through their patrons and leaders within the power structure, *futebol* appears to provide the setting for experiencing the 'horizontalisation of power' through the reification of a sport. Thus, it is in this way only that the people can virtually 'see' and 'speak' directly to 'Brazil'. It is through *futebol*, then, that the masses are also permitted an intimacy with the national symbols. It is only on the days when the all-Brazilian team play, that one can observe the people dressed in the colours of the national flag, living out a physical experience of the union of and with the nation. In these moments of a 'civic *carnaval*' created by *futebol*, all sacred symbols of the fatherland, whose use is ordinarily limited by regulations in Brazil, cease to be the property of representatives of the dominating segments and are shared among the anonymous masses who celebrate a relationship of frank and uninhibited intimacy with these symbols.

(b) Rules in opposition to groups and individuals

When *futebol* is discussed in Brazil, an outstanding aspect of this sport is the acceptance of the rules of the game as an immutable, and above all, unquestionable system. In other words, it is a system which is above the reach of the political, religious or economic power of the clubs or teams so that they have to accept victory or defeat with the same so-called Olympian spirit. As we say in Brazil, *devem saber perder e ter espírito esportivo* ('they must know how to lose and have a sporting spirit'). Despite these thoughts, we still may allocate the responsibility for the defeat on a referee, linesman or some player. The ease with which we assign social responsibilities in such a personal way also occurs in a witchcraft system (*cf.* Gluckman 1972), and seems to be correlated with the presence of a rigid set of fixed, immutable rules. When such rules exist, it is then much easier to find a person who becomes the outstanding star of the victory or, on the contrary, the scapegoat for the defeat. Frequently, this figure is the referee who interpreted or applied a rule of the game incorrectly, but it also can be a certain player.

But *saber perder* (to know how to lose) means to accept social equality as a basic axiom of the game without which it becomes impossible to think about the very idea of games. As Lévi-Strauss indicated in a famous passage, the basic idea in games is that the notion of equality exists when the contest begins. For it is this equality between teams that should be transformed during the course of the match, resulting, by the end of the game, in inequality and, therefore, in a discontinuity between the teams (*cf.* Lévi-Strauss 1962, Chap. 1). It is necessary to observe, nevertheless, that games can only operate institutionally when both parties are in agreement about their eventual differentiation into victorious or defeated teams. In this way, equality before the rules is the main element in the structure of games, an aspect which is profoundly different from the general structure of rituals where the officiant has more knowledge of the rules of the supernatural than does the client for whom he is carrying out the rite. Thus, this basic equality of games—where all are under the rule of the same rules—stands in opposition to the authority and the basic inequality of rituals—where the priest and the 'rules' are one and the same, in opposition to the congregation.

Remembering this, it will not surprise us to learn that the beginnings of sports as a mobilising activity of both national and international, human and material resources, is parallel to the birth of the modern, egalitarian and individualistic society. That is—and this is well worth adding—it is parallel to the development of a social order founded on the recognition that universal laws are applicable to all individuals. In contrast, one of the distinctive aspects of traditional societies is that inequality is seen as something natural.[4] A result of the institutionalisation of inequality at all levels is the multiplicity of legal and judicial systems existing in the same society. Consequently, in traditional societies, the same crime committed by people located in different social levels was judged in a different way. This orientation constitutes the 'regime of privilege' or of private law.

The institutionalisation of a sporting contest in the modern world is a direct function of the vigour of the universal rules to which everybody submits themselves. This acceptance, in my view, is one of the most basic aspects of sports as a modern activity, for competition cannot exist without it. On the other hand, this acceptance of rules that are both unique and universal merely amounts to a reproduction, at the level of another domain, of the bourgeois ethic, according to which 'everyone is equal before the law' and the market.

In the Brazilian case, we know that this juridical equality is a point of tension between groups and that vestiges of the traditional order still exist in Brazil. For example, military personnel and professional liberals, have the right to claim a 'special prison' when they commit crimes, not to mention rights accepted as legitimate and granted to relatives of persons occupying positions of prestige and power. In fact, one of the major dilemmas of Brazil is the tension between a system of personal relationships which guarantee the existence of hierarchies, favours and privileges, and a set of modern universal laws which guarantee the opposite, since they are based on equality (*cf.* DaMatta 1979).

Soccer as exemplary of fairness

My thesis is that in such societies, the popularity of sports like *futebol* lies in the capacity of the sport to provide a special experience with permanent structures, defined through universal rules which govern the game and that nobody can modify. Now, this is in quite a contrast with what happens in many other domains of Brazilian society, where the mere possibility of defeat is enough for the dominant groups to seek to modify the rules of the game. But soccer, this humble instrument thought to mystify the masses, provides an exemplary experience of respect for the law. Here, laws cannot be changed so that everybody is truly equal on a soccer field during a match. Victory is the reward that will actually be received by the team which plays better.

As has been observed, we have been considering *futebol* as an instrument which lets us practise a necessarily open and highly democratic form of equality since it is based on performance. Again, this differs from the usual procedures of classification where people are defined through their relationships (belonging to a family, having an important friend, working for some powerful person, etc.) or by some physical attribute like the colour of their skin. In *futebol*, and in popular recreational activities in general, classifications are made according to performance; that is, they are made on an individual basis. Thus, nobody can be proclaimed a *futebol* star by his family or godfather because he must prove his qualities through public demonstrations. It is a test which is very rare in Brazilian society where a hierarchy sets up everything in a place and *quem é bom já nasce feito* (whoever is good was born that way).

In this highly hierarchical milieu, the 'space' created by *futebol* (and by other recreational events such as *carnaval* and certain forms of popular religion) provides the possibility for the existence of individualised and free expression through which anybody can show himself as he is, with all his abilities and weakness, without imperiling his network of personal relationships. The fundamental point I wish to demonstrate here is the structural tie between the possibilities for individual expression and certain domains of Brazilian society. What has been verified, as I have previously stated in other places (DaMatta 1979, 1986, 1987), is that the chance to win through merit and performance only occurs in areas such as *futebol*, *samba*, *carnaval* and the popular religions and arts in general.

These considerations bring us to another very important point. If *carnaval*, popular religiosity, and *futebol* are so basic in Brazil, then everything indicates that, quite in contrast with certain countries of Europe and North America, the sources of our social identity are not the central institutions of the Brazilian nation such as the constitution, the national congress, the university system, financial order, etc. Rather, they are made by these recreational activities which in the central and dominant countries of Western civilisation are secondary and certainly limited sources for the creation of solidarity and social identity. Thus, it is music, hospitality, friendship, relationships with saints and spirits, and naturally *carnaval* and *futebol* which lets the Brazilian enter into contact with the enduring aspects of his social world.

Thus, beyond being a sport, *futebol* in Brazil is a basic vehicle of socialisation and a complex system for the communication of essential values in a highly segmented society (Vogel 1982). It is also a domain in which dominated segments of the society can search and be assured of a basic ideological continuity. Whereas the form of the constitution and government change constantly and the monetary system, universities and political parties only raise doubts for Brazilians about whether or not they really have a modern nation, *futebol*, *carnaval* and personal relationships portray Brazilian society as great, creative and generous, having—like the soccer played in the country—a most glorious future.

Notes

1. A complete version of this essay will be found in *Universo do Futebol* (Rio de Janeiro 1982). A summarised version appeared in *Le Débat* 19 (February 1982).
2. Mário Filho, author of a solitary study on the position of the negro in Brazilian soccer, says of this event: 'The proof (of our defeat in 1950) would lie in these carefully picked out scapegoats who are by coincidence all black: Barbosa, Juvenal and Bigode. The white players from the Brazilian team were not blamed for anything.' It is clear that they were selected precisely because they were black.

Furthermore, they were also playing in the defence line of the Brazilian team. We know that in the case of defeat, it is usual to blame the defence. In the case of victory, the situation tends to be reversed.

3. See the hyper-nationalistic article by Otto Lara Rezende, entitled: 'Brasil bola Brasil-Pelé pátria Pelé', published on the occasion of the conquering of the Third World Soccer Cup by Brazil, in *Jornal do Brasil* (20 June 1970).

4. See the works of Louis Dumont given in the bibliography for fundamental considerations along these lines.

References

DaMatta, Roberto, *Carnavais, Malandros e Heróis: para uma Sociologia do Dilema Brasileiro* (Rio de Janeiro 1979); *O que faz o brasil, Brasil?* (Rio de Janeiro 1986); *A Casa & a Rua* (Rio de Janeiro 1987).

Dumont, Louis, *Homo Hierarchichus: The Caste System and its Implications* (Chicago 1970); *Religion, Politics and History in India* (New York 1970).

Gluckman, Max, *An Analysis of a Social Situation in Modern Zululand* (Manchester 1958); 'Moral Crises: Magical and Secular Solutions', in *The Allocation of Responsibility* (Manchester 1972).

Guedes, Simoni Lahud, *O futebol Brasileiro: Instituição Zero*. MA dissertation, Programa de Pós-Graduação em Antropologia Social do Museu Nacional (Rio de Janeiro 1977).

Lévi-Strauss, Claude, *La Pensée Sauvage* (Paris 1962).

Mário Filho, *O Negro no futebol Brasileiro* (Rio de Janeiro 1964).

Sahlins, Marshall, *Culture and Practical Reason* (Chicago/London 1976); 'Culture as Protein and Profit', *The New York Review of Books*, 23 November 1978.

Turner, Victor, *Schism and Continuity in an African Society: a Study of Ndembu Village Life* (Manchester 1957); *Dramas, Fields and Metaphors: Symbolic Action in Human Society* (Ithaca/London 1974).

Vogel, Arno, 'O Momento Feliz', in *Universo do Futebol* (Rio de Janeiro 1982).

Bruce Kidd

Canada's National Game

CANADIAN ICE hockey is a classic example of a 'national game'. While Canadians play and watch a great variety of sports, hockey is our great passion, our self-defining liturgical drama. I bear witness as a lifelong participant. Nothing else matches it for dramatic pull and pleasure. It gives us our most popular heroes, our most accessible myths and rituals. To learn it is to enter the society. Other peoples have played stickball games on ice, but the modern variant is our very own, codified in the commercial cities of central Canada and elaborated and loved on rinks and riverbeds across the land. Although today it's mostly played on machine-made ice in heated arenas, it evokes the settlers' triumph over the harsh, northern climate. As Roland Barthes (1961) once observed,

Man has taken the elements of immobile winter,
the frozen land, and suspended life,
and fashioned them into a rapid, vigorous, passionate sport.

In the metaphorical season of death, our forefathers created the dance of life itself. We take its growing international popularity as a tribute to their genius.

Like other 'national' sports, hockey gives Canadians our most Durkheimian moments of communion. No other cultural activity unites so many—patrician and punker, scholar and schoolgirl, tenth-generation Quebecois and last year's Asian immigrant—in common purpose and celebration. During the depression, when the population numbered just over twelve million, an estimated eight million persons—two out of every three men, women and children—tuned into a playoff game. In more recent years, when the national team plays the Soviets, the entire country seems to shut down to watch. The representational status of the players draws much of its power from the collective nature of the enterprise. As anyone who has ever shovelled a slough or flooded a rink well knows, just getting started is usually a social labour. The vast network of teams and leagues today depends upon expensive public facilities and millions of hours of paid and volunteer labour. Successful teams have become surrogates for entire towns, cities, regions, and the two constituent nationalities of French- and English-speaking Canada. When all these communities are drawn together behind Team Canada, it's a powerful moment of national awareness. Although it was almost two decades ago, virtually everyone alive at the time can still tell you where she or he was when Paul Henderson scored the winning goal in the 1972 series against the Soviets. The celebrations gave stirring reinforcement to the pan-Canadian project—undertakings and institutions defined along national lines.

But as other articles in this special issue of *Concilium* argue, the nature and extent of opportunities and the cultural meanings expressed are inextricably bound up with the social formation in which sports are played. Under some circumstances, a 'national sport' can undermine desirable undertakings. In the case of hockey, the game's great potential for self-empowering, socially affirming physical education and cultural expression has been distorted by a hegemonic masculinity which champions brute strength and the violent acting out of anger over intelligence, grace, and humane social relations. At the same time, its power of national validation is often frustrated, if not effectively blocked, by the continentalist sports media complex which controls it. As a result, community-responsive and externally-dominated structures and progressive and dehumanising meanings are continually at odds: for most of its history, the game has been a site of deep cultural conflict. This turn of affairs, and the current possibilities for corrective intervention, are the subject of this article.

1. The quest for a 'national game'

Harnessing sports to nationalism has been a goal of Canadian sports leaders since the beginnings of the modern practice in the mid-nineteenth century. The men who established the first clubs, formal rules, and governing bodies—the petit-bourgeois professionals, small businessmen and civil servants of cities like Montreal—were ardent supporters of the Confederation project and the dream of a vibrant, new independent nation. Many of them worked in the commercial enterprises which hoped to prosper from the vast internal trade opened up by western expansion. Long before their activities spread beyond Montreal and southern Ontario, they claimed 'national' status for them, staging 'national' championships and keeping 'national' records. They also sought to combat the popularity of other cultures' sports—particularly English cricket and American baseball—by creating distinctively Canadian ones (Gruneau 1983).

The first was lacrosse, developed from the widely played Amerindian game in the years immediately prior to Confederation by the Montreal dentist George Beers. Beers promoted lacrosse so aggressively that there are many today who believe he persuaded the new Parliament to declare it 'the national game'. (He tried, but was unsuccessful.) Although the game enjoyed great popularity for the rest of the century, lacrosse never gained a foothold outside the Montreal-Windsor corridor and lower British Columbia, and was in general decline by the First World War. Scholars offer several explanations, from the increasingly violent play to the game's strong association with the native peoples at a time of growing racism. Another candidate for the mantle of 'national game' was Canadian football, with a structure somewhat in between British rugby and the American code. But football began as the game of the elite boys' schools and universities. Initially, it had few working-class or francophone adherents and easterners and westerners fought bitterly over the rules. After the turn of the century, when it did begin to draw large audiences, many teams 'imported' Americans to play for them (Cosentino 1969). It could never carry the full burden of national representation. Hockey, the youngest of the major team sports, quickly outdistanced them all.

But hockey has had its divisions, too, particularly along ideological grounds. The game's first organisers were patriarchal amateurs in the improving tradition of 'rational recreation', who pursued 'the making of men' and the amelioration of class conflict through the provision of opportunities. They soon found themselves in conflict with municipal boosters prepared to recruit and pay players in the interests of a winning 'community' team (in the tradition of British soccer) and outright entrepreneurs who sought to package and sell the game for profit maximisation (in the tradition of American baseball). These differences proved irreconcilable. In the years prior to the First World War, the amateur bodies repeatedly rejected any accommodation with professionalism. The sport was irrevocably split into amateur and entrepreneurial sectors, with those advocating a limited professionalism in the community interest forced to choose sides. On the one hand was the Canadian Amateur Hockey Association (CAHA), on the other several small, struggling capitalist leagues, of which the three-team Pacific Coast

League and the four-team National Hockey League (NHL) were the most stable (Metcalfe 1987).

Up until the late 1920s, the amateurs held the upper hand. The CAHA controlled a coast-to-coast network of teams and leagues and arguably the best players. It also enjoyed the largest audiences and the greatest public prestige. For many, amateurism still connoted an idealistic, public-spirited approach to life. It had not become the pejorative it is today. But in a few short years, the NHL entrepreneurs gained practical and ideological domination of all Canadian hockey and restructured it along continentalist lines. Their triumph has frustrated the nationalist ambitions of hockey lovers to this day.

2. Continental capitalism

In retrospect, the early successes of the strict amateur faction proved to be their undoing. The lack of a supportive Canadian base turned the entrepreneurs to the United States, where larger and richer markets, the relative weakness of the amateur tradition and the post-war economic boom created favourable conditions for rapid expansion. Between 1924 and 1926, the NHL entrepreneurs swallowed up—and closed down—their western Canadian competitors and added six new US franchises. (The depression would reduce these to four, but the Canadian franchises were reduced to two, so US owners retained the majority.) Although themselves primarily from the petit-bourgeoisie, they increasingly took on corporate partners. These steps gave them access to much greater capital and revenues than ever before, and a tremendous advantage in any bidding for players. At the same time, they benefited from—and shrewdly contributed to—the growing legitimisation of professionalism which took place in step with the world-wide spread of commercial culture. (Kidd and Macfarlane 1972).

A crucial step in this process was their capture of the new state-owned national radio network—the Canadian Broadcasting Corporation (CBC)—for the exclusive broadcast of their own games (and the advertising of their prime sponsor, the Standard Oil subsidiary, Esso). By the mid-1930s, the Saturday evening 'Hockey Night in Canada' enjoyed the highest ratings in the land. Despite the great popularity of many CAHA teams, 'Hockey Night in Canada' always featured NHL games, usually those played by its Toronto franchise, the Maple Leafs. As commentators frequently exclaimed at the time (e.g. Selke 1962), the broadcasts changed changing popular loyalties overnight. In the late 1930s, the CAHA fought back, legalising professionalism and aggressively competing with the NHL for players and Canadian fans. But world war ended the 'hockey war'. While the six-team

NHL maintained operations, the far-flung CAHA was devastated by enlistments and the outmigration from smaller centres accelerated by the mobilisation. In 1947, it was forced to sign an unconditional surrender, becoming an elaborate NHL farm system (Canada 1967). Given the capitalist league's superior financial and ideological resources—their consolidation of what scholars call a 'sports-media complex'—and the continentalist commodification of all cultural forms, it would have been difficult for the CAHA otherwise to have reversed their declining fortunes. However, we should not regard their defeat as inevitable, but contingent upon specific historical decisions and circumstances.

3. Impotent nationalism

Canadians have continued their love affair with hockey throughout the long post-war period of NHL domination. The League's successful television version of 'Hockey Night in Canada' has had much to do with its lasting popularity, and the 'conversion' of immigrants and successive generations. It has undoubtedly brought much pleasure to millions. But rather than reinforce proud images of national well-being and independence, NHL hockey underscores dependent continentalist (and metropolitan) ones. Although five Canadian cities received new franchises in the 1970s, the majority of teams (presently 14 of 21) continue to be located in the United States. As most of the players are Canadian, this arrangement ideologically naturalises the process by which the bright and gifted are forced to sell their labour in a richer society elsewhere. It's most poignant when Canadian children transfer their day-dreams to American cities in this way.

The NHL has repeatedly thwarted efforts to place strong Canadian teams in international or Olympic competition. In the 1950s and 1960s, when CAHA teams represented Canada in international competition, it continually bought away the best players, even when they were of no immediate use to NHL teams. In 1970, in an effort to bring the NHL 'on-side', the CAHA relinquished control over Canada's international teams to a new body, Hockey Canada, which the Canadian government had created to strengthen Canadian performances, but the NHL only agreed to participate if its interests would be kept paramount. In 1972, despite Prime Minister Trudeau's personal appeal, it barred four players from the national team chosen to play the Soviets because they had jumped to a rival league. Except for the quadriennial Canada Cup competitions, in which the NHL stars are encouraged to participate, the League gives only limited assistance to the national team. (A noted exception is the Calgary franchise, which operates in the not-for-profit tradition of the earlier 'community professional' teams.) When the pan-Canadian representative cannot be composed of 'our best', it suggests the futility of nationally focused undertakings.

Against those who believe sports should contribute to humane cultural expression and self-development, the NHL proudly displays a masculinity of brutish anti-intellectualism. Largely because its executives have believed that physical intimidation and fighting are part of the game's attractions, they have encouraged the unsupportable idea that fighting is a 'natural' outlet for frustrations, and that it's an act of cowardice (rather than intelligent self-discipline) for a 'man' not to physically defend himself when provoked. The great Wayne Gretzky is still widely slandered as a 'wimp' because he refuses to fight. The message for females is that they need not apply. Largely because they believe that frequent game-playing best prepares a young athlete for the rigours of the $80+$-game NHL schedule, they have created an apprenticeship system (in junior leagues outside the school system) which makes it all but impossible for the young player simultaneously to pursue an education. Despite its many resources, the NHL has contributed very little to the sport sciences and the development of coaching. Instead, it teaches an unthinking obedience to managerial authority, no matter how crazed or immoral. This, too, undermines the constituency for the 'national game'.

4. Community resistance

To be sure, corporate control and the sorry practices it has encouraged are widely resented and resisted, particularly on the issues of 'hockey violence' and players' education. Stimulated by teacher, parent, and general public concern, the CAHA and federal and provincial governments have combined to create a humanistic certification program for volunteer coaches. In a number of communities, organisers have developed innovative 'fair play' campaigns and have restructured the game to encourage skill and enjoyment, rather than 'win-at-all-costs'. Despite the persistent belief that hockey is the quintessential 'man's game', girls and women have won themselves new opportunities. But despite the support of a few noted players for these efforts, little change is evident in the upper levels controlled by the NHL.

Given its enormous modelling and symbolic power (Smith 1983), it's important that the struggle to recapture popular control be taken to the NHL as well. In radio and television, film, and book publishing—other important spheres of culture which have been dominated by foreign corporations—Canadian governments regulate commercial activity and/or subsidise Canadian-based efforts, in an effort to keep cultural expression and distribution in Canadian hands, so an obvious question is why not hockey, too? Yet few governments have dared interfere with—let alone dismantle—the most powerful monopolies, such as the American-controlled film distributorships and the NHL. In these neo-conservative times, with a Free Trade Agreement now in effect with the United States, more vigorous intervention in the interests of 'Canadian culture' will be even harder to obtain. But if there was a political will, effective instruments are there, because the NHL-media complex is so highly centralised. It would be quite feasible, for example, through the regulatory Canadian Radio Television Commission and the CBC, to change the dominant interpretation of 'Hockey Night in Canada'. (At present, it is still controlled by the League and its sponsors.)

There ought to be the political will, because 'national sport' has become self-reinforcing national metaphor. An independent society should have its best cultural creation within its own control.

References

Barthes, R., 'Of sport and men' (National Film Board production script). (Montreal 1961).

Canada, Report of the Hockey Study Committee of the National Advisory Council on Fitness and Amateur Sport (Ottawa 1967).

Cosentino, F., *Canadian Football* (Toronto 1961).

Gruneau, R., *Class, Sports and Social Development* (Amherst 1983).

Kidd, B. and Macfarlane, J., *The Death of Hockey* (Toronto 1972).

Metcalfe, A., *Canada Learns to Play* (Toronto 1987).

Selke, F., *Behind the Cheering* (Toronto 1962).

Smith, M., *Violence and Sport* (Toronto 1983).

PART III

Sport: Ethics and Religion

Dietmar Mieth

The Ethics of Sport

1. The discernment, development and intensification of moral insights in sport

FINDING OUT what is morally right is the work of reason. It is also a matter of rational choice between various possible judgments about the predictable consequences which something or other might have for human beings. Moreover, establishing what is ethically proper involves different levels of human experience, which are also interrelated in the context of religious experience.

The latter setting is more appropriate for the development of religious ethics. This article, however, is not about substantiating behavioural rules in sport, where we may doubt that religious ethics has any specific contribution to make. In fact, the debate about a normative sports morality is now part of what is universally accepted as ethics grounded on reason without any special religious considerations. That is a procedure quite acceptable to theologians and wholly applicable to sport.

This article, however, is concerned with what might be called 'preventative sets', or 'virtues', which have to be established in the context of contrastive experience: in the midst, that is, of an actuality with negative emphases.

Contrastive experience starts from existing potentialities which have been inadequately perceived hitherto. Hence it may also be thought of positively as the discernment of possibilities. It is not, however, yet another constraint to add to the existing array.

(a) Sport as a means of being human: finding a balance between development and abstention

(i) Everyday experience shows that personalities can develop specifically in sport. One of the possibilities of sport is taking part in a learning process. If morality, as tradition unanimously maintains, depends on volition, then the metaphor behind Nietzche's punning references to the 'exercise of the will' is relevant here. The exercise of the will is an asceticism which finds its anthropological yardstick in a human volition purged of self-concern. Asceticism is purified self-love.

This learning process includes self-distancing and restraint as an inward aspect of specific development. A further essential characteristic is moderation as an expression of practical de-ideologisation. Anyone concerned to discover what is appropriate to him or her is also looking for a progressive equilibrium of individual potentialities, which have to be made to develop reciprocally.

(ii) Sport as a means of being human has something to do with the nature of the 'social character' (Erich Fromm) which it produces. By this I do not mean temperament but the effects of an assimilation process of the world and a socialisation process between human beings. The notion that development through sport, and ultimately sporting achievement, presupposes character is as important as the idea that it helps to produce it. It should be clear that the development of sport depends on the human context.

In regard to sport as a mode of being human, the means should not be confused with the end. Instead it shows the way, and its goal is not the activity itself but something outside it. According to Fromm, there are two possible social characters: one has a destructive and the other a productive orientation. The destructive tendency may also be seen as a product-orientation. It makes everything human approximate to the inanimate and dead, which in the end is spiritually destructive. The productive tendency, or *biophilia*, on the other hand, does not see the result of a performance as an outline or as a thing, but is interested in how the activity helps to transform the human being himself or herself.[1]

(b) From fairness to justice. The development of the sense of justice (Rawls)[2]

On the one hand, 'fairness' comprises personal dignity: that is, the inalienability, uniqueness and individual purposiveness of persons. On the other hand, fairness also comprises traditional ideas of *aequitas*, of equity, of a balance of presuppositions, requirements and possibilities. Fair behaviour is equivalent to the one, and fair rules are equivalent to the other. Whoever wishes to be fair and just and needs corresponding rules to be so, has to make principles of equality the basis of developing freedom, and therefore has to accept the precedence of equality over freedom.

According to Rawls, however, the most important practical rule of the sense of justice is the 'maximin' principle. This is a criterion for the establishment of rules which serves and determines the thrust of justice, so that every measure (we hope) is directed to the greatest advantage (maximum) of the most disadvantaged (minimum). This criterion is unusual for us, for our society by reason of economy is used to an emphatically utilitarian philosophy. A utilitarian attitude sees a measure as just if the disadvantages of certain groups can be set against the advantages of the whole.

In accordance with this maximin criterion, it is possible to decide whether priorities in rule interpretation, priorities in sport promotion, priorities in environmental justice, and priorities of self-control in sport are just and fair.

(c) Solidarity and liberation

The ethics of sport is often subject to the paradigm of self-realisation, which together with a possible restriction of claims is often met in encounter with other persons. From this viewpoint, the social dimension is ultimately an external 'imperative of avoidance'. But a constructive social emphasis would assume that sport is also thought of politically. Discussion of the so-called politicisation of sport often 'barks up the wrong tree', even though it rightly rejects inappropriate political functionalisations of sport. From the ethical standpoint, however, the false aspect of politicisation is not the transposition of sport into the political dimension, but unjustifiable political application of a political phenomenon. Anyone who, like Vatican II, would conceive sport as a contribution to the establishment of fraternal relations between people of all conditions of life, nations and races,[3] will necessarily advocate a 'political' sport. The political dimension includes on the one hand the public character of sport, and on the other hand responsible involvement with social institutions. Sport is a public social institution. Involvement with it belongs to the realm of political ethics.

Accordingly, a lot depends on the ethical question, 'What is the point of sport?', rather than on the question of what politics can do for sport, which is, so to speak, a political oasis. Not only justice, but the principles of solidarity and liberation have to be considered here. These principles permit an association of sports ethics and political ethics. The attainment of solidarity is a presupposition of sport itself and of involvement in sport: for access to solidarity means the simultaneous learning of restriction and of openness. Solidarity mediates between the need for reciprocal partisanship and the drive to continual extension of this option.

The concept of liberation is a more astonishing adjunct of sport, perhaps. Yet, from a politico-ethical viewpoint, it is important for sport to make the transition from paradigm of imperial development aid (or, as we might term it, structural promotion), to paradigm of self-reliance in a context of liberation. Sport should be communicated politically, for it is a cultural phenomenon, but it should be subject to emancipatory processes.

(d) Sport is an amoral concept.

Its moral relevance is decided in practice. Perhaps there will once again be cultures in which people survive without sport and possibly live better lives without it. Nothing entitles us to assume that our cultural activity 'sport' is more than the result of specific social processes, the ultimate meaning of which cannot be assessed as yet. In this sense, sport is not a supra-temporal but an historical 'good'. It is subject, in fact, to a form of historical necessity which neither society nor the individual can easily avoid but must make the best of.

Sport is a leisure pursuit, an achievement pursuit, a mode of obedience to the drive to self-display, a means for young people to meet on a supra-national level, and a means of symbolic cultural exchange. It is all these things, which all have possible ethical implications, especially the international youth movement and symbolic cultural exchange.

Sport has even been called a form of peace movement in itself. That is excessive and obscures the difference between non-moral values or commodities, and moral values which indicate the criteria for use of such commodities. For example: sport serves peace as a process of reduction of force and of inducement to social justice, when it is practised appropriately. In fact, it can be put entirely in the service of the opposite of peace: it can be used as a part of the athletic armoury of different political blocs, as a nationalistic self-enhancement, as a glorification of competitive ideology, as aggressive potential, and as a form of utilitarianism (the end justifies the means).

Admittedly, sport politics in the context of political ethics can be tantamount to peace politics, and the pursuit of sport can adopt some of the learning processes proper to peace education. Precisely in this regard, sport is ethically relevant only if it is a task and no more than that. It has no ethical dimension as a triumphalist declaration of ownership.

2. Does sport in society have a reductive effect on human beings?

Sport in or as a social context does not mean that sport is one among other areas of life, but that the imbuing of human beings in society with sport is a form of 'inflexional language' or, as Luhmann has it, a form of 'reduced complexity' in social life. It is a language which a human being has to use in this particular way, even when apparently avoiding this specific area of life. Such avoidance is possible however only as a conscious refusal which is systematically and appropriately integrated into a sports context, as something 'unsporting' (which nowadays is much worse than being 'unmusical').

If we accept that sport is a social context or social system in the sense of a form of reduced complexity of the world of life, it seems appropriate to consider this reduction in an environmentally 'critical' manner: that is, from the viewpoint of a 'human' environment. Then we must take the multiplicity of possible human images into account. Accordingly, I see the Christian view of humanity as an 'open concept' which comprises consistency in terms of a living tradition, and the equilibration of actual areas of human life. Therefore the following observations seem apposite:

(a) The reduction of physicality to the level of physical culture

The Fathers of the Church supported two extreme tendencies in the Christian critique of the inadequate integration of physicality in sport in classical antiquity. There was the 'Apollonian' separation of spirit from body, and the 'Dionysian' separation of the body from spirit; that is, the body as an instrument of idolatry. The Old and New Testaments accord here with the Fathers: games are idolatry, which Tertullian says the baptised must shun. Clement of Alexandria anticipated the judgment of the twentieth-century Church with a more nuanced opinion: physical culture yes; sheer physical culture no. (Pius XII)[4] This discernment of spirits demands closer consideration.

Physicality is reduced to the level of physical culture when, for example:
(i) the health of a human being is seen as a purely physical thing. Psychosomatics long ago told us that health is unattainable by isolating the body. If however the illusion is pursued that health is a purely physical functioning of the body, then physicality is an inadequate way of representing the whole human being;
(ii) when human physicality is confined entirely to the ideal of the body trained in sport. Advertising and everyday notions of appropriateness in regard to the appearance of the body, in fashion for instance, but also in

normative distinctions between the sexes, confirm the ideal of a body transformed by sport. Historically speaking, this form of reductionism was not always self-evident, as Rubens' paintings show;

(iii) when functional pleasure and readiness for play as forms of expressive physicality are unilaterally converted into an image of physical achievement. The onesidedness of sporting achievement is more liable to harm than to promote a holistic view of body nurture. Examples of this tendency are tennis elbow, cyclist's cramp and excessively pronounced weight-lifter's muscles;

(iv) when the training of the body associated with sport interrupts youthful physical development, or when sport so to speak exacts its price of a delayed injury which shows its negative effects in old age if not before.

Of course these known critical aspects do not mean that human beings cannot and do not have to live with reductive features in their lives, on condition however that they also observe the principles of moral integration: that is, the release of reduction from mere partial goals, from, in fact, reductions. They also have to keep to the motto 'nothing to excess', which was Johann Michael Sailer's contribution to the debate.[5]

The social problem of physicality resides in its instrumentalisation. Long ago so-called 'games' became mere performances in which only success counts, and participation, always in question with mass sport, itself represents success on the potential achievement scale. How magnificent to be one of the 80,000 who were allowed to take part in the New York marathon! The imbuing of life with sport is not a physicalisation of life, but a progressive cerebralisation: that is, the drive to achieve is ultimately located in the brain. Therefore it is scarcely surprising that in achievement sport the successful are those who can train their brains.

(b) The reduction of the play element by achievement culture

For some time now the social symbolism of sport, even of broad-based sport, has been located not in physical culture but in achievement culture. Krokow put it this way: sport expresses the principles of industrial society better than that society itself.[6] Sport without something to be counted and assessed is mere play or even 'idle' art. The sporting person is the prototype of success. The achievement principle of modern society means: human equality and inequality depend on the individual. Each person can be the architect of his or her own glory.

It is a sporting maxim that taking part is more important then winning. I have already remarked that this is useless when participation itself is a symbol of success. It would only be possible to return sport to the human level of play if sport were pursued for the sake of play: that is, when playing is more important than winning. But this would mean a change in social behaviour in respect of sport. Unfortunately the public do not think that playing is more important than winning.

In itself play is meaningful communicative movement. That is how Vatican II sees it in its Pastoral Constitution. In itself sport is meaningful communicative movement.[7] But the achievement culture is a reduction of communication to the level of consumption of results. The alternation of remembering and forgetting for the sportsman—producer and consumer— is characteristic of that. The modern human being has to 'train' for the play element in sport.

Of course performance and play should not be forced into an absolute antithesis. The language of play must comprise the language of performance. The reductionism of performance culture in sport is directly hierarchical: that is, result-oriented performance decides the permissible elements of play.

(c) The reduction of communication to the level of consumption

In Christian social ethics, the *ordo rerum* must remain subordinate to the *ordo personarum*. The personal element, or, in terms of social psychology, human identity, also includes subsistence or, in chronological terms, consistency and communication. In Christian tradition the person is not unrelational but becomes a self through relationships, and therefore in a communicative process.

Sport is wholly a locus of communication. A series of sets of movements, which give sport its expressive power, may be interpreted as a kind of pre-linguistic or unique linguistic communication. This is true of sport itself, above all of team sport, but also on the periphery of sport. The more sport comes under the rule of goals, success and achievement, the more one-dimensional is the possible communication of the participants, and the more it obeys the will to achievement of the industrial society or of the performance society. Everyone does his or her job.

In my opinion communication and ethics form a hermeneutical circle: that is, they mutually presuppose one another. This hermeneutical circle makes it rather difficult to distinguish between descriptive levels: between, that is, the observed communication of social mediation processes, and the valuative level, where it is decided that communication is always desirable.

Let us try the descriptive level first. The area of life known as sport represents a relatively independent system of social mediation processes, and also a relatively autonomous system of linguistic and specialist communication. If that communication is essentially performance-oriented in the sense of success and result, then communication as a form of accounting predominates. Just think of the mass media.

The counterpart of sport as a form of result-oriented communication is a result-oriented communication for the sake of sport. This is associated with acceptance behaviour. Sport-related consumer behaviour reduces social sensitivity to the result. For the critical observer, all that counts is the tension which occurs between result and performance.

The imbuing of society with sport gives rise to the sport-consumer mentality, to the consumption of results. Here consumption also has a surrogate function: the possibility of living by proxy.

3. Ethical problems of the commercialisation of sport

(a) Developments and phenomena

The collective term 'commercialisation' comprises quite different phenomena and developments, which ultimately result in a progressive interaction of economy and sport as leisure and achievement behaviour. That includes the industry of sports equipment and clothing and the construction of sports locations and the financing of sporting events, the establishment and maintenance of sport organisations and divisions, and the use of sport and sports information for publicity purposes, outside and inside the sport industry, and for the financing of promotions, premiums, compensatory payments, retainers and prize money, and the economic administration of sports manufacturers and their means of production.

(i) In general, the economisation of politics and everyday life is a growing tendency (which also means the politicisation of the economy). At the same time, under the pressure of the unequal division of labour, there is an increase in performance profiles and achievement behaviour. The mutual approximation of top professional sport and broad-based sport as far as performance level and awareness of demands are concerned, means that the economisation of sport is the result of a general social development, and not an exception which can somehow be ignored.

(ii) Economisation is a consequence of the growth system. The transition from quantitative growth to qualitative growth has been as little evident hitherto as the realisation of an equilibrated economy that would obey the rules of energy saving, environmental protection and just distribution.[8] The need for economic expansion is evident everywhere in society. Science and technology develop essentially as functions of this need (*cf.* media development, microbiology).

The expansion of economic structures and economically conditioned behaviour into sport is, so to speak, enforced. The sporting performance which has its 'reward' in the non-economic sector (health, the discovery of identity, social communication and recognition), gives way to a form of sport which, beyond the non-economic reward, brings payments in money or other economically convertible tokens. The sport which occurs in a non-purposeful setting of mere joy in play and communication, gives way to the demands of increased turnover (publicity, marketing): that is, it is subordinate to the economic accounting of events. Leisure sport is increasingly subject to the influence of the products which, in the shape of sports equipment, sports stadia and so on, as well as sports clothing, make it more effective and at the same time aid the laws of performance and competition. Anyone who falls back and stays behind materially in the main areas of mass sport (skiing, tennis) cannot keep up and is no longer in the line for non-economic 'rewards'.

(iii) The resistance of sporting organisations on the various regional, national and international levels to these developments decreases as, in addition to compulsory economisation (and internationally the distinctions between social orders play no part here as long as only growth economies are concerned), the professionalisation of sport increases ineluctably. This professionalisation has nothing to do with the special conditions of top professional sport but has resulted from training, organisation and care in mass sport. Anyone who says 'A', that is, who is favourable to the imbuing of society with sport and to the democratisation of sporting possibilities, also has to say 'B': that is, has to take sport increasingly into account as a vocational service. Naturally the consequence of this is that sport as a social service, and sport as an economic exploitation process of capital and labour, progressively reduce the social part-autonomy of sport and become a factor of integration in universal social developments, in which a Nobel Prize, victory at Wimbledon and exporting a record number of motor cars have the same economic symbolic effect.

(iv) The economically and socially conditioned decrease of the partial autonomy of sport, however it offends against the notions of a 'wholesome world' of sport and is restricted to speeches, is to be explained as a system-environment relationship. The more the selective elements of the system decrease under environmental influences, the more the system adapts to general needs and expectations, which in their turn underlie the more global form of system control. Instead of the area-specific profile, there is an increased tendency to level down at the orders of economisation, so that sport performance, the production of entertainment and scientific efficiency, and even the evangelisation of churches must obey the same rules.

(v) Such developments can be limited by various forces, whose stability is of course exposed to the constant pressure of development: by the declaration of the partial autonomy of the sub-system in accordance with selective rules whose validity it demands for itself; by social forces which act in the name of non-economic human values and developments or obey them at least partially; by state influence, which ensures the 'freedom' of sport as much as the freedom of art and science: this is, by management of the significance of the economic valuation of products and achievements.

(vi) The commercialisation of sport depends not least of all on the fact that sport *inter alia*, but increasingly, is a mass media product which is to be marketed universally almost immediately, so that sport is subject to the dual rules of its own self-regulation on the one hand and its external regulation as a media commodity on the other. The more the system of sport and the mass media system are mutually involved, the more dependent they become on one another and the greater the danger that sport communication will become the mere equivalence of two economic interest camps, still without any role being accorded to consideration of 'the specific values of sport (apart perhaps from the peripheral area of fatal collisions).

(vii) The greater the economicisation of sport the more the dimension of sport becomes peripheral, and the more non-economic needs and values (which do not have to be ethical values in and for themselves) are forced from the centre to the periphery of sport.

(b) Economicisation and commercialisation: discerning spirits

Hitherto I have discussed phenomena and developments in respect of the general problem. Now I must discover some criteria for making distinctions and proceed from their basis.

(i) First of all it is necessary to establish how far the economicisation of sport answers (a) sport goals; (b) social needs and (c) material needs. This would be tantamount to a search for the correct extent of a (qualitative) economicisation of sport.

(ii) Secondly, we have to work out where the economicisation of sport debouches into its commercialisation; that is, where it becomes a commodity rather than obeying its true nature. Here I used economicisation in the negative sense of commercialisation. Here the same criteria apply: the commercialisation of sport occurs when (a) economicisation takes place at the expense of sporting ends and means; (b) at the cost of social needs and value-orientations; and (c) with a reduction of special needs.

It seems to me that these distinctions could still be made in the pre-ethical area, if the presupposition were accepted that sport possessed its own value and an associated partial autonomy; that is, sport is not allowed to masquerade in the commodity role of an economic valuation process.

The distinctions become more debatable when for sport ethical criteria (representing an ethically appropriate concern with the values of sport) are to be brought into the context of universal socio-ethical notions (of, say, Christian social teaching) for the discernment of spirits.

(iii) Then it is a question (in the third instance) not only of the restriction of commercialisation within the setting of a compulsory economicisation, but of the limitation of *homo oeconomicus* by means of a holistic conception of human beings pure and simple. That requires the introduction of positive criteria: (a) a non-economic form of human dignity; the revaluation of non-economic needs and corresponding value orientations or basic attitudes; (c) the proposal not only of personal but of structural alternatives to the developments described.

The use of such criteria is certainly possible only in discussions with experts from other disciplines or with some other form of practical experience. In the following, therefore, I shall mention only a few examples which might help to explain the relevant criteria more effectively.

(i) Appropriate economicisation

(a) Aims of sport are, for instance, exercise, training in movement, pleasure in achievement, personal relations and social recognition. Economic means and economically responsible planning are necessary to promote these goals. In so far as free economic forces co-operate in the promotion of these goals while furthering their own interests, their efficiency must also be assessed in regard to these aims.

(b) Social needs are, for instance, help for the socially disadvantaged (*e.g.* sport for the handicapped, structural aid to rural areas or new urban housing projects) and an absence of information. Here too it is possible to accommodate particular economic interests (all the more so if work can also be provided). Here it is a question of balancing ends against means.

(c) Material demands include, for instance, more professionalism in training, recreation and organisation. Here, in addition to balancing ends against means, it is also a matter of support, bringing influence to bear and balancing interests.

(ii) Discerning negative aspects of commercialisation:

(a) At the expense of sporting goals and aims: if, instead of exercise, body culture, play, and achievement, the main concern is with the entertainment of spectators; if direct human contact is lost in favour of the isolation of individual performances; if the formation of a sports élite loses contact with the basis; if the commercialisation of the promotion of achievement uses impermissible means (stress and damage to health; the use of questionable drugs); if sports medicine becomes more important than training; and so on.

(b) At the expense of social needs and valuations: if the maintenance and origin of other leisure and cultural values are impaired; if the promotion of sport in events and broadcasts leads to competition with other needs (care for the family, personal interests); if industrial concerns promote sport but omit to humanise the workplace; if sport and care for the environment are made to compete, and so forth.

(c) By altering the degree of material necessity: if it is only the market value of performance in sport seen as a commodity which determines its reward instead of the achievement itself, and the appropriate needs of the sports person; if the sports organisation, bureaucracy, and information function solely in accordance with commercial demands; if professionalisation sees its task as primarily one of serving the interests of competitive achievement and not as the increase of other sporting goals; in short: if commerce decides the aims of sport instead of the other way round.

(iii) Favourable criteria for orientation to human dignity

(a) Since human dignity is not decided by economic ends (even though it requires economic means), the following criteria have to be observed:

—human self-determination (*e.g.* should parents and educators mark out children as future sportsmen and sportswomen?);

—fundamental human needs (in addition to basic physiological needs, the need for personal relations, social recognition, and meaning: should success in sport downgrade superior needs?);

—individual and social rights (*e.g.* the right to appropriate education, to the opportunity to choose one's vocation, to work as a fundamental principle of self-realisation, and so on);

—humanity as a self-explanatory goal in human relations (how far does commercialisation threaten human relations, inasmuch as one's fellow human being becomes no more than a means to winning?).

(b) Value-orientation and basic attitudes: if sport is to help make possible a 'productive' (Fromm) human orientation (in contrast to a 'destructive' orientation), then the following criteria have to be observed:

—justice as fairness;

—the capacity for self-restriction;

—the promotion of life and environmental justice;
—the potentiality of peace.[9]

Such values can only be aimed at if human needs remain uncommercialised.

(c) Structural alternatives: here it is a matter of establishing due proportions between the relevant criterion, the means used, and the goals of human success, not by appealing solely to the individual sports-people affected but as a way of promoting the structural conditions of 'rational' sports persons. Such considerations come to the fore in utopias, such as an anti- or alternative Olympics. Perhaps there are less complicated instances—unfortunately any more detailed account is beyond my competence. Nevertheless I can envisage a reduction of the unilaterality of sport by a constant introduction of new events (one example would be the union of Langlauf and slalom in competitive skiing).

The foregoing are merely experimental illustrations of the relevant criteria. The moral theologian can do no more than suggest possible criteria; he cannot provide actual solutions.

Translated by J. G. Cumming

Notes

1. *Cf.* R. Funk, *Mut zum Menschen: Erich Fromms Denken und Werk* (Stuttgart 1978).
2. *Cf.* J. Rawls, *A Theory of Justice* (Oxford 1972); *id.*, *The Liberal Theory of Justice* (Cambridge, Mass. 1973); O. Höffe (ed.), *über John Rawls 'Theorie der Gerechtigkeit'* (Frankfurt am Main 1977); *id.* (ed.) *John Rawls, Gerechtigkeit als Fairness* (Freiburg/Munich 1977).
3. *Gaudium et spes* (1965), 61.
4. See Tertullian, *De spectaculis 4* (*Selected Writings*, Vol. 1, Munich 1912, pp. 108, 124ff.; 128ff. = *Bibliothek der Kirchenväter*, ed. O. Bardenhewer *et al.*, Vol. 7); Clement of Alexandria, *Paidagogos* 3, 9–10 (*cf.* A. Koch, *Die Leibesübungen im Urteil der antiken und frühchristlichen Anthropologie*, Schorndorf 1965, pp. 84ff.); on Pius XII, *cf.* A. F. Utz and J. F. Groner (eds.), *Aufbau und Entfaltung des gesellschaftlichen Lebens: Soziale Summe Pius XII*, 3 vols. (Fribourg 1954–61), Nos 2016; 2044–2067; 5129–5146.
5. See J. M. Sailer, *über Erziehung für Erzieher* (Munich, 2nd ed. 1809) pp. 248–251.
6. *Cf.* C. Graf von Krokow, *Sport und Industriegesellschaft* (Munich 1971); W. Hädecke, 'Leistungssport und Leistungsgesellschaft' in *Grenzen der Leistung* (Olten 1975), pp. 134–146.
7. *Ibid.*

8. H. C. Binswanger *et al.*, *Wege aus der Wohlstandsfalle. Der NAWU-Report. Strategien gegen Arbeitslosigkeit und Umweltzerstörung* (Frankfurt 1979).
9. *Cf.* D. Mieth, *Die neuen Tugenden* (Düsseldorf 1984), pp. 107–141.

Sean Freyne

Early Christianity and the Greek Athletic Ideal

WITH THE confidence of a true Hellene Plato declares that the barbarians do no engage in sport or philosophy. Yet the same author has his master, Socrates, suggest that the only 'penalty' he has incurred for his philosophising is to be maintained by the state like the victors of Olympia (*Apology* 35b). There was for some at least in the ancient world a distinction to be made between these two hallmarks of the Greek way of life—philosophy and sport. The early Christian apologists were anxious to appropriate the former as an accurate designation of their own belief-system; there was a much greater hesitation about any contact with the latter, despite its popular appeal with the masses. Why this hesitation and does it afford Christians with a suitable criterion for evaluating involvement with athletic pursuits today?

An adequate answer to this question can best be provided by a consideration of the role of the athletic ideal in the Greco-Roman world generally, as well as by an examination of Jewish attitudes towards this essentially Greek pursuit within that culture. The early Christians in other aspects of their lives were able to assimilate elements from both these 'great traditions', while making a distinctive statement in such areas as ethics, liturgy, administration, literary fashions and the like. What of the athletic ideal and whence the hesitancy that may be detected to the very end of the late antique period? As Chrysostom wryly remarks: 'If you ask Christians who is Amos or Obadiah, how many apostles there were or prophets, they stand mute; but if you ask them about the horses or drivers they answer with more solemnity than rhetors (*Homily* 58).

1. Ambivalence towards the athletic ideal in Greek culture

Pindar, Strabo and Pausanias all ascribe the origins of the Olympic games to Heracles, the human who in Greek mythology had become divine through his labours.[1] By proving their prowess in sporting events young men (for the most part) exemplified something of the power of the divine in bodily form. Allowing for the poetic genre, Pindar's odes, celebrating the victors in the games, express this point of view most clearly. The ideal athlete was profiled differently at various times, yet the virtues that are called for reflect clearly what the Greek city demanded of its citizens in order to ensure its continued stability: 'perfection, physical beauty, wonderful condition, mighty skill, irresistible strength, daring, rivalry, indomitable resolution and inexpressible ardour for victory' (Lucian, *Anacharsis*, 12).

It is not surprising, therefore, that Plato gives such a prominent role to athletic training for his ideal city. Unlike the poets who should be banished because of their subversive activities, athletes brought honour to their city, reflecting the actual situation in Greece where Olympic victors were provided for and had certain rights even outside their native city. Thus, according to Plato, gymnastics (*i.e.* athletic training) should be treated on a par with music (*i.e.* the liberal arts), provided a proper balance was maintained. Women too, should receive such training. Contrary to prevailing practice, which apparently excluded women from Olympia except on certain days, Plato has an enlightened view, seeing the issue of nudity (the normal condition of the athlete in competitions) as secondary to the fact that men and women shared the same nature and both could equally act as guardians of the city (*Republic* Bk II, 376e; Bk V, 457a–b).

This position already points to the beginnings of criticism of the athletic ideal that was becoming an end in itself, due to the increased professionalism. For Plato, the one who concentrated on gymnastics alone in their education ended as 'a hater of philosophy, uncivilised, never using the weapons of persuasion'. Aristotle, too, though recognising the scientific nature of athletics, is conscious of the excesses that can occur. In his day, professionalism, special diet and other tactics meant that success was possible only for the few, in contrast to olden times when all could aspire to victory (*Nicomachean Ethics*). Euripides is even still more scathing. 'Although there are myriads of evils throughout Greece, there is nothing worse than the race of athletes', he declares. The criticism is levelled against the special position that was awarded the athlete in the city life, which in the view of Euripides, was not warranted. It is not the athletic victor, but the wise and the good who should receive garlands since it is they who rid the city of evil, 'putting an end to strife by their wise counsel' (*Autolycus* Fragment 282).

The Greek passion for athletic contests may not have captured the imagination of the Romans to the same extent as other aspects of the 'captive's' way of life. Nevertheless, the philosophic critique of the athletic ideal continued in Rome also. Seneca would exclude gymnastics entirely from his liberal curriculum. 'For what is there "liberal" about the students of these subjects who are ravenous takers of emetics, whose bodies are fat while their minds are emaciated and torpid?' he asks contemptuously, (*Letters* 89 18). Pliny the Elder wanted all contests banned from Rome, and Plutarch, a Greek who came to live there, explained Roman suspicion of athletics as follows; 'They (the Romans) are of the opinion that the gymnasium and the *palaestra* are more to blame than anything else for the slavishness and effeminacy of the Greeks ... and that it was these which produced restless idleness in the cities, immorality and the ruin of young men's physique with naps, strolls, rhythmic exercises and exact diets' (*Roman Questions* 40).

2. Jewish attitudes towards athletics

It must be emphasised that this strand of philosophic criticism of the Greek athletic ideal did not greatly alter the popular perception of the athletic contest. With the increased professionalism and the spread of Greek ways beyond the mainland, especially in the east after Alexander's conquests, we hear of athletic contests far from their natural homeland, even in Jerusalem itself (2 Macc. 4:10–14). Thus the Greek way of life in general proved attractive in cultures such as that of the Jews where previously there had been no tradition of such activities. In the meantime the old Olympian games languished for want of money as the athletes flocked to games elsewhere in search of more lucrative prizes. It was thus that Herod the Great, ever anxious to be seen as the supporter of the hellenistic spirit, found himself appointed president of the Olympic games in 12 BC since he was prepared to act as their patron.

Deep-seated attitudes arising from a different world view as well as historical circumstances meant that for religious Jews of the Hellenistic age, certain expressions of the Greek way of life such as the gymnasium, the theatre and philosophy, were totally unacceptable. For the author of Second Maccabees, as well as for Josephus the establishment of the gymnasium in Jerusalem was a departure from ancestral customs. Many aspects were operative—nudity, the religious associations of the games for the Greeks as well as the introduction of graven images.

One can understand the sharp Jewish reaction at the time of the hellenistic reform of Antiochus IV in the mid-second century BC, since the thoroughly hellenised high priest, Jason, was quite prepared to see the Greek way of life corrode the distinctive Jewish faith, even to the point of sending money from the Jerusalem temple for the support of the quadrennial games at Tyre (2 Macc. 4:18). Almost a century and a half later (28 BC), Herod the Great had no such intentions in organising games in honour of the emperor at Jerusalem, since his purpose was rather political, by showing himself to be both a loyal servant of Rome as well as an able administrator within his own kingdom. These games were not, therefore, intended as a sacred contest and Herod made sure that the amphitheatre was located outside the precincts of the city.[2]

Nevertheless, these Jerusalem games occasioned violent Jewish reaction, despite the fact that other Jews appear to have actually participated in the events. An attempt on Herod's life failed, but the opposition succeeded in causing a general uproar, thereby disrupting the games and ensuring that subsequently they were held at Sebaste, not Jerusalem (*Jewish Antiquities* 15:267–279). The opposition was undoubtedly religious. Athletic contests had had distinctively religious associations from the beginning in Greece, as the first recorded account, the funeral games for Patrocolus (Homer *Iliad* Bk. XXIII, 256–897), as well as the archaeological evidence from Olympia and elsewhere makes abundantly clear.[3] In Roman times, this was further accentuated by the use of the games to honour the Emperor, something that strict Jewish monotheism could not easily accommodate, in view of the suggestion of emperor worship. In such a context images of various kinds only helped to foster further the anxieties of the more strict Jews that presence at such events was a form of idolatory.

3. The early Christians and the Greek athletic ideal

There was then plenty of precedent for early Christian reluctance to engage in athletic contests of various kinds. The philosophic tradition had transferred the notion of the true contest (*agon*) to the sphere of the ethical struggle in which those who sought to live the good life were engaged, and the victor's crown was seen as properly belonging to the philosopher/sage, following the Platonic ideal. Jewish monotheistic reserve also provided a model of resistence that in time led paradoxically to Christians, not just not participating in games, but becoming victims in the gladiatorial contests that were a particular feature of the games in Roman times.

There is little indication of this in the pages of the New Testament. The Acts of the Apostles gives some hints of the new movement's less than friendly encounter with the educational and commercial life of the Greek city (Acts 17; 19), but the world of the games does not intrude itself into the picture. The parables of Jesus reflect the variegated social and economic life of Galilee, yet there is not even an allusion to the athletic arena. Josephus informs us that there was a stadium at Tiberias and a hippodrome at Tarichaeae, both, significantly, Herodian centres. The liklihood would seem to be, that Jesus avoided such centres entirely, as also Sepphoris, rather than that he visited them only to be rejected. Accordingly, neither Jesus nor his followers came from that echelon of Galilean life that might have been attracted to such centres, it would seem. Thus, while many of Jesus' images are drawn from the world of Galilee, they are taken from those aspects of that life that his audiences would have shared, and these did not include either the arena or the *palaestrum* which were more likely to have been frequented by those Jews who found the Herodian cities attractive.

It is at Corinth that we find the clearest reference to Greek athletics in the early Christian literature. This is only as we would expect in view of the city's close association with the Isthmian games in honour of Poseidon, one of the four great festivals held regularly in mainland Greece. 'Do you not know,' Paul asks rhetorically, 'that in a race all the runners compete, but only one receives the prize?' (1 Cor. 9:24).[4]

This allusion, descriptive though it be of the arena, is suggested to Paul by the overall context of the discussion, namely, the relative rights and responsibilities of the weak and the strong on the issue of meat sacrificed to idols, which presumably became more readily available in the markets at the times of the great festival. Paul concludes his argument about freedom and responsibility by discussing his own example of refusing to accept payment for apostolic services, though technically entitled to it because of the dominical saying about the labourer being worthy of his hire. There would appear to be an implied contrast with the professional athletes of his day, only too ready to accept the lucrative prizes that were on offer irrespective of the circumstances of their victory.

A lot has been made of Paul's accurate information of the arena and the *palaestrum* (where the boxing and wrestling events took place) in this and other allusions scattered throughout his letters (1 Thess. 2:19; Gal. 2:2; Phil. 3:13; 4:1; Col. 2:18; Eph. 6:12; *cf.* also 1 Tim. 4:7; 2 Tim. 2:5; 4:7). It has even been suggested that this knowledge goes back to his youth at Tarsus, where, according to Strabo, athletic contests were held in which Paul himself may have competed as a middle-distance runner, because of his short stature![5] One could equally well claim that these passing references were simply the reflection of Paul's desire to be 'all things to all men' as part of his missionary strategy. As we saw already, the transference of the idea of the contest to the moral life was a well established *topos* among the Greek moralists. Indeed, by comparison with the Stoic moralist, Epictetus, or the Alexandrian Jew, Philo, Paul's athletic allusions are quite sparse and passing, showing none of the detailed knowledge or sustained comparison of Philo in particular. More vivid descriptions such as 'pommelling my body' or 'straining for what lies ahead' (1 Cor. 9:27; Phil. 3:13) are few. Theologically inspired language such as crucifying oneself, or metaphors taken from the cultic or military spheres appear to be just as natural and suited for his purpose of highlighting the sacrificial nature of the Christian life, as Paul understood it. (See Rom. 12:1; Eph. 6:10–12).

In one important respect Paul's imagery was to prove highly significant, namely the claiming of a higher crown of victory than humans could offer (1 Cor. 9:25). Jewish monotheism had prepared the way for resistance to participation in the athletic festivals because of the dangers of idolatory. Throughout the second century Christians were faced with difficult choices with the increased emphasis on the emperor cult, especially in the east, in conjunction with athletic festivals and other spectacles, often sponsored by the Emperor himself. People such as Cyprian of Carthage, himself an educated Greek, before his conversion, afterwards warned of the crudity and dangers of such contests and gladiatorial shows, eventually earning for himself the martyr's crown, but also the acclaim of the pagan mob. Some bishops, such as Gregory of Pontus, initiated celebration of the martyrs as a way of countering the attraction of athletic festivals for the masses. It would appear to be no accident, as Robin Lane-Fox notes, that throughout the third century coins, papyri and inscriptions show an increased concern with athletic contests of various kinds in those very regions where the Christians were being persecuted. This renewal of the Greek way of life was an attempt by the old aristocracy to turn the clock back and counter the barbarians at the borders.[6] Because of their lack of support for this cultural restoration, Christians were viewed as the enemy within. Yet, for them, the idea of the martyr's crown had been too firmly established to be bartered for mere earthly honours.

It is not at all clear what, if any, direct influence the conversion of Constantine had on the nature or continuation of athletic festivals. The final days of Olympic contests are uncertain. According to the eleventh-century chronicler, Georgias, the final Olympiad fell in the age of Theodosius the Great (392–5). This, however, does not mean that Christian propoganda had prevailed, since the great festival had encountered increasing difficulty for some considerable time, even before the Christian era. Contests continued at Antioch until the sixth century, despite the best efforts of Chrysostom to divert the minds of the masses to 'higher things' in his day. The story recounted by Jerome of Hilarion of Gaza blessing a successful charioteer reflects a more realistic appraisal of the situation that Chrysostom's strictures. (*Vita Hil.*) Once the idolatrous connotations were removed there seems to have been little principled Christian opposition to athletic and other contests as such, and their popular appeal with the masses, especially chariot races, can be seen from the social role of the charioteer as late as sixth-century Byzantium.[7]

4. Conclusion

This discussion of early Christain attitudes to the Greek athletic ideal has pointed to the social as well as to the religious significance of the games in antiquity. On the one hand the Christians were anxious to be seen to take a full part in Greco-Roman society, yet in certain aspects there could not be, nor was there, any compromise. The idea of 'the third race' was no mere slogan and the religious context as well as the political and ideological use of games, especially in imperial times, meant that this was one area of real confrontation in terms of that wider culture. Christians were fortunate that despite Plato's call for a balance between physical and philosophical education, the ancient ideal had been badly damaged over the centuries. This was the direct result of the professionalism and elitism of the athletic guilds, often under powerful patronage. Thus, the criticism was already well formulated and the transference of the metaphors of the arena to other spheres of life was a well-established strategy. Nor should one neglect the influence of the Jewish rejection of the idolatrous associations either, even when many, Jews and Christians, undoubtedly shared the popular enthusiasm for the contests and the shows.

In attempting to formulate an adequately critical attitude toward contemporary sporting contests, therefore, it is important for Christian theologians to evaluate their social as well as their cultural significance. Because of its popular appeal and claims to human excellence, sport has always been threatened by ideological abuse and personal greed. There is nothing in the authentic Christian tradition that is negative to sport as such, but there is much there to warn us to be constantly critical of its abuse.

Notes

1. For a convenient collection of the relevant ancient texts see Rachel Sargent Robinson, *Sources for the History of Greek Athletics* (Cincinatti 1955). See also Wendy J. Raschke, *The Archaeology of the Olympics: The Olympics and Other Festivals in Antiquity* (Wisconsin 1986).

Wendy J. Raschke, *The Archaeology of the Olympics: The Olympics and Other Festivals in Antiquity* (Wisconsin 1986).

2. For a detailed discussion see M. Lämmer, 'Griechische Wettkämpfe in Jerusalem und ihre politischen Hinttergründe', *Kölner Beiträsge zur Sportswissenschaft* 2 (1973) 182–227.

3. D. Sansone, *Greek Athletics and the Genesis of Sport* (Berkeley 1986), attempts to explain the origins of all sports as a ritual sacrifice of human energy with its origins in pre-historic times when man was a hunter. The theory is perhaps too elaborate, and fails to take account of the special features of Greek sport, especially the concentration on the victor and the privileged place that is given to him in Greek culture.

4. See O. Broneer, 'The Apostle Paul and the Isthmian Games', *Biblical Archaeologist* 25 (1962) 2–31.

5. H. A. Harris, *Greek Athletics and the Jews* (Cardiff 1976).

6. R. Lane-Fox, *Pagans and Christians* (Harmondsworth 1987) pp. 537f.

7. Y. Dan, 'Circus Factions (Blues and Greens) in Byzantine Palestine', in L. Levine, ed., *Jerusalem Cathedra* (1981) pp. 105–119.

Jürgen Moltmann

Olympia Between Politics and Religion

OLYMPIA IS continually in the throes of a political crisis. Do these crises mean the end of the Olympic games? Is the Olympic idea running aground on the political realities? Many people in many different countries are beset by these doubts. And they are right. Yet every crisis is also a chance. As soon as we realise that the paths we have pursued hitherto do not lead any further, we have to start out afresh. But we can only find the way out of a crisis if we trace it back to its foundations, and renew ourselves from our own foundations as well. This seems to me the great—indeed the unique—chance offered by the present crisis of the Olympic games: it is an incentive to think through the Olympic idea once more, to understand it better, and to uphold it more consistently than has been done in the past.

Many sportsmen and sportswomen, and many sports federations, feel that they are the innocent victims of political manipulations which prevented them from taking part in the Olympic games in Moscow or Seoul. They are quite right. Sport has a dimension of its own—its own particular experience of life and happiness—which is not identical with the political dimension, and which really is therefore misappropiated if it is subjected to political interests and considerations. But at the same time we have to recognise that the modern Olympic idea was a political one from the very beginning.

1. Olympia as a religion

The founder of the Olympia idea, Pierre de Coubertin, talked about sport's 'detachment' from commerce and politics; yet at the same time even he already linked it with two political concerns.[1] First of all there was an internal political concern—what he considered to be 'the enormously soothing, pacifying power of sport' in social conflicts. Public sport acts as a 'social lightning conductor'. It becomes 'a link between the different social classes'. In the common rejoicing over a victor or a victorious team, a collective identification is born. Social differences and conflicts recede behind the spontaneous feeling: '*We've* won!'. But of course public sport does not abolish social conflicts. It merely blurs the conflict between the classes. It stablilises the social order – and the social disorder. And it is precisely this which it is supposed to do, in Coubertin's view.

Secondly, there is an external concern: 'the honour of our country'. In ancient Olympia, victories were a sign of the favour of the gods, but modern Olympic victories reflect national glory. 'Anyone who participates in the games exalts his country and his race by so doing', said Coubertin. The participants should remember that their efforts are 'on their country's behalf'. The superiority of a country's sportsmen and sportswomen is to prove the superiority of its political system, we are told in declarations made in the socialist countries. 'We have to regain our Olympic superiority', urged Robert Kennedy in 1960, speaking for the United States. Sporting triumphs are then viewed as the yardstick showing how much a nation counts in the world, and what its economic system can achieve.

All this shows that from the very beginning the modern Olympic idea involved the estrangement of sport from its own particular experience of life. By coupling world sport with national susceptibilities and emotions, Coubertin also surrendered that sport to the national conflicts between the different states. Like many nineteenth-century humanists, he believed in 'a harmony of nationalisms'. Meanwhile—although Coubertin was not yet in a position to see this—the conflicts between nation states have turned into world-wide conflicts between capitalism, socialism and the Third World. And these conflicts are also and inevitably the conflicts in which the Olympic games are caught up today.

If we look back to the beginning of the modern Olympic idea, we have to ask the critical question whether the national organisation of the Olympic games serves the sportsmanship of sport, or is its downfall.

If we look back to the beginnings of the modern Olympic idea, we have to ask, further, whether the social and psychological function of the Olympic games as sport geared to sensational triumphs has not distorted these 'games' into the performance struggle of professionals in the political interest. Are the Olympic games really still games at all? Are they in fact playful? Do they give pleasure? And when we ask which countries can afford to act as host for the games, we find ourselves in the exclusive circle of the wealthy nations.

Behind the political and economic crisis of the Olympic games, the moral crisis of today's world is obvious to every eye. The classic ideals of humanity which are inextricably bound up with the Olympic idea are immediately disavowed the moment that the interests of the major nations are affected. Is this the old familiar conflict between high ideals and shabby political realities? If it were, then the Olympic idea would simply be sharing the fate of all good ideas. But the moral crisis of politics today has in fact to do with something different: it is a matter of short-term and long-term goals. The political conflicts about Afghanistan, and the resulting boycott of the games by the Western nations in 1984, were short-term. But in the long term the concern for world peace can only be guaranteed—however laborious the process—by way of a world-wide community of nations. This is not just an idealistic notion. It is the realistic condition for humanity's survival.

The Olympic idea is in reality part of this necessary idea of the world-wide community to come. When the Olympic games suffer, the world-wide community suffers. If the Olympic idea dies, this is an indication that our future is dying. In view of this fact, did it make sense to subordinate the long-term political concern for this future of the whole of humanity to the short-term interests of one's own nation, and to dispense with one of the few places where people can meet together on the way to this world-wide community?

Even in the universal moral crisis which also manifests itself in the Olympic games today, we have to go back to the origin of the Olympic idea itself if we want to take the opportunity to revive and renew it. This idea has been echoed and re-echoed ever since Coubertin. Is it capable of showing us a way into the future? Coubertin crowned the modern Olympic idea with his notions about the *religio athletae*. The 'religion of sport' was intended to bind the nations together and was to be the preparation for the future 'world religion'. He saw this religion as 'a declaration of confidence in the future'.

But all over the world today confidence in the future has turned into anxiety. This is the deepest crisis of all. For anxiety in the present makes people and nations blind to the future. General anxiety kills the future before ever it is born. From what religious sources can the Olympic idea be reborn to new strength? Coubertin found it necessary to crown the Olympic idea with the Olympic religion because without religion the idea would lack dynamic force, enthusiasm and the quality of the absolute. In ancient times, religion really was the driving power behind the peaceful athletic struggle. Religion was the moral authority on which it rested, and the forum for the whole Olympic festival. The games were part of the Greek religion, for the

Greek religion was a religion of festival. Religion led the way. The games followed.

In the modern Olympic idea things seem to be reversed. The religion has become part of the games. It was invented because it was required. So the modern *religio athletae* has become nothing more than a synthetic product.

Coubertin himself was a free-thinker and had no intention of founding a new religion. No one was supposed to give up his own religion in order to participate in the new Olympic one. The idea was rather that the new Olympic religion would bring peace to all the rival religions of the world.

Coubertin therefore took over from the ancient Olympic religion only its useful rituals, not its gods. The place where the games took place was to be a 'sacred precinct', a 'place of pilgrimage'. The entry of the athletes was to be a 'procession', the Olympic committee a 'college of priests', the Olympic oath a purifying rite, the victory ceremony a homage of the nations. A throng of artists were to make of the games a religious festival. 'In Olympia', he said, 'people gathered both for a pilgrimage into the past and for a declaration of confidence in the future. This would really be just as appropriate for the revived Olympics.' Coubertin also wanted to fill these old and new religious rituals with a common religious élan which was to bind the nations together. By this he meant a spirit which would rouse enthusiasm, and which was symbolised by the Olympic flame. For him Olympia was more than an organisation. 'The first and essential characteristic of both the old Olympianism and the new is that it is a religion', he said in 1935.

As the 'Ode to Sport' shows, the new Olympic sport is glorified as a 'gift of the gods', as 'king', and as 'divine'. Because Coubertin took over from the old and new religions of the world only their rituals and emotions but not their gods, sport itself, the participants in the games, the people, the nations, and ultimately humanity must themselves become the content of the modern Olympic religion: 'Rejoice in the continual revival of humanity!'

The German Olympic mentor Carl Diem stressed the *humanitas athletae* in the *religio athletae*: for him Olympianism was a 'solemnly idealistic and humanist emotion', which through the games was 'to raise the human race, split up as it is into so many different religious creeds, through a common concept of pure humanity.'[2] Olympia awakens a true 'attitude of peace' and sets 'world brotherhood' tangibly before our eyes. For Carl Diem too, the Olympic ceremony meant 'consecration'. The Olympic games are 'the day of faith in the sacred springtime of the nations'. That is why the Ode to Joy from Beethoven's ninth symphony formed the climax of the Olympic liturgy in Berlin in 1936.

Avery Brundage, for many years president of the international Olympic committee, made himself the prophet of this new religion in 1964, at the opening of the sixty-second session of the IOC. The Olympic movement, he said, was a twentieth-century religion, a religion with a universal appeal, which united in itself all the basic values of other religions. It was a modern, exciting, vital, dynamic religion, attractive to young people—and the members of the IOC were its prophets. Here were none of the injustices of caste, class, family or money. 'In the field of sport', Brundage declared, 'everyone stands or falls according to his own performance.'[3] Is there any proof of this? Brundage justified his religious feeling about Olympia in 1969 when he said: 'When you remember that 114 teams marched into the Olympic stadium in Mexico City teams in which all races, all colours, every religion and every political opinion was represented, capitalists and socialists, royalists, fascists and communists—all marching behind the Olympic flag with its five rings, not because they were forced to do so, but because this was their own desire—then I think I may maintain that nothing like it had ever happened before' (*Der Spiegel* 52/1969).

We continually come across hymns of praise like this about the Olympic religion, or about sport as the religion of the world. They are to be found everywhere. Up to now they have never been subjected to any fundamental criticism; nor have they been properly assessed. Either this religious aspect of Coubertin's Olympic idea is taboo in Olympic circles, or it is simply not taken seriously. But the crisis which the Olympic games are going through today enjoins a public discussion of this inner religious dimension of the games too, and makes us ask about its weaknesses and its renewal.

2. Olympia as play

Theologians and atheists schooled in the criticism of ideologies and religions find no difficulty in criticising the new Olympic religion. To read the solemn ceremonial speeches closely is to recognise the directing minds behind the Olympic games. The ironic impression that comes across is that Feuerbach has acted as ghost writer and that the scenario was composed by Marx. For this modern Olympic religion really is wishful thinking, a dream fantasy, opium for the people. It is a dangerous glorification of sport and a deification of the games which deprives both sport and games of their humanity. *Cui bono?* Who profits when sport and play are elevated to the solemn and lofty level of a religion? Certainly not the participants, who take pleasure in the sport and the play. It benefits only those who wish to use the games and their participants for extraneous purposes. Coubertin did not start from any of the familiar religions of the world. His point of departure was religious patriotism, his aim being to press forward to Olympic internationalism.

It is immediately obvious that Olympia as a religion is an idolatry. Religious Olympianism might even be viewed as the classic example of an artificially constructed modern worship of false gods. The robes in which these idols are clothed are borrowed from other religions, especially the European ones. The religious symbols and rituals are not original. They are second-hand. The Olympic games are no longer arranged in honour of religion; the religion is got up in honour of the Olympic games. The religious emotions and energies of the masses are now chanelled towards a different object; for in Olympia human beings extol themselves, adore themselves, sacrifice themselves and reward themselves. A religion without God leads to the idolising of human beings and their achievements. But the idolisation of human beings puts a strain on those human beings which is greater than they can bear, and thus makes for inhumanity.

Religion is never, ever, purely beneficent. It is always and everywhere dangerous as well. This being so, we have to ask the advocates of the modern Olympic religion whether with their religious consecration they have not always deprived sport and play of its human quality. Of course people need the religious element in life. But what is left of a religion if it is made the means to an end? What happens to it then is just what happened to sport when it is used as the means to a political end: it becomes a deadly danger, like everything which it degrades and misuses.

Yet in spite of this criticism of the Olympic religion, there is something inherent in the Olympic experience and the Olympic idea which this criticism cannot destroy—something which, on the contrary, the criticism wishes to set free. This element is the truly religious dimension of life, liberty and joy.[4] I should like to illustrate it from two different phenomena.

The first is the simple and quite fundamental human pleasure in sport, the satisfaction over a successful sporting achievement, and the happiness given by a successful game. Sport and play have belonged to human beings from the very beginning. They are part of what it means to be human. In sport human beings find themselves, discover their strength, sense their limitations. They play with their physical potentialities and give their lives form and organisation. In play a person discovers his attitude to other people, and gives the community he shares with them form and organisation. Sport and play have a significance of their own for the becoming-human of the human being. They have their own dignity and their own inherent meaning.

In sport and play human beings do not aim to produce anything. They wish only to act themselves out. Here they are artists, not technicians. They do not manufacture anything utilitarian; they present something that gives pleasure. When people see themselves as free and wish to make use of their freedom, then what they do is play, said Schiller. It is this non-utilitarian yet inherently meaningful dimension of play which is sport's truly religious dimension. Sport for the sake of one's country, or in honour of socialism, or as a supreme achievement of capitalist meritocracy—these are alienations, misuses and obliterations of the fundamental human dimension of sport, which is therefore the truly religious one. The person who rides in the Olympic games ought not to 'ride for Great Britain' or the United States or Germany. He ought to ride because he enjoys riding, and rides well. It is highly desirable, and indeed necessary, for the Olympic committee to reformulate the Olympic idea so as to preserve the humanity of sport and promote the liberty of play.

The second phenomenon is the hope for freedom which is inherent in the original experience of sport and play, and which Coubertin also rightly perceived and aptly formulated. Every religion is ambivalent. It can be opium for the people, and it can be a ferment of liberty. Criticism of the new Olympic religion is useful if it destroys the opium and brings out the ferment of liberty. Olympia really will be 'a declaration of confidence in the future' if the games are no longer put on in such a way that they 'pacify' social conflicts and shroud political disputes in oblivion. Olympia has a great potential for protest—protest against the economic exploitation of men and women, protest against racist humiliation, protest against the masculine depreciation of women, and protest against the nationalist barriers between human beings. In Olympic sport and the Olympic games the participants in themselves already present a world of peaceful competition, mutual recognition and friendship which offers an alternative to the real world in which we live and from which we suffer. Are the Olympic games not preludes of hope for a successful, harmonious life among human beings everywhere? They are preludes of this kind for everyone who can play, and wants to play. Olympia will be 'a symbol of hope' if its character as protest, as alternative, and as the prelude to freedom is stressed, in its contrast to burdened everyday life in the economic, political and social world. This is a primal human longing. It has a religious dimension because in it men and women experience their 'ultimate concern' (in Tillich's phrase) and something that continually gives them pleasure. The Olympic religion must revert to this element of hope, which is its natural element. It is highly desirable, and indeed necessary, for the Olympic committee to protect this hope for liberty from its political, social and economic misuse.

3. Olympia as alternative

The Olympic games are going through a crisis today because from the very beginning the Olympic idea was in a special sense political. As I see it, the only way out is for the Olympia idea to be given back to the original experience of sport and the original hope of play, and for it to be reborn from these things. The Olympic idea itself must not involve the alienation of sport and the manipulation of the games for some extraneous purpose. The Olympic idea must ensure that the Olympic experience is shielded from exploitation by other interests. Here the following points seem to me to be worth discussing:

— The Olympic religion can change from a solemn glorification of sport and an ideal dream fantasy into a ferment of liberty in this world of enmity and oppression. It will then bring the original Olympic experience to bear on these alienated experiences of life.

— Public sport, especially world-wide Olympic sport, is onlooker sport. That is a fact. But it must not be a substitute for the onlooker's lack of sporting experience. Sport can also be presented as an incentive to active personal experience. This is the function of Olympic education.

— The national basis of the modern Olympic games is no longer tenable in this age of political blocs. Participants are no longer motivated by patriotism, and patriotism is hardly now promoted by participation. Would it make sense for the organisation of the Olympic games to be more closely linked with the UN? Would it not make sense for the games to be financed by a UN fund? Would it not make sense for victories to be celebrated as the victories of individuals, not nations? Olympia would become a sign of hope if it became the concern of men and women, not merely the concern of nations—and the wealthy nations at that, for the most part.

— Sport and games are based on a way of life, and present a special way of living. The modern commercialisation of public sport has made it a matter of performance, and a commodity. And by so doing it has destroyed sport's own life-style. Should the Olympic idea not be in a position to remove the Olympic games from performance and consumer thinking, linking the games with a simple way of living which would liberate people from this meritocratic and consumer society of ours? Coubertin favoured the idea of an ascetic way of life. Today this is more than the virtue of sportsmen and sportswomen. The life-style of the coming world-wide community can only be that of a simple and a common life.

Olympia as the expression and reflection of our divided, oppressed and threatened world is in a crisis. Olympia as an alternative of community in this divided word, as an alternative of liberation in this oppressed world, and as an alternative of life in this threated world: that is our chance in the crisis.

Translated by Margaret Kohl

Notes

1. Pierre de Coubertin, *L'Idée Olympique. Discours et essais* (Stuttgart 1966) (ET *The Olympic Idea. Discourses and Essays*, trans. J. G. Dixon, Lausanne and Stuttgart 1966); also his *Mémoires Olympique* (Lausanne 1931), and his *Oeuvres Complétes* 7 vols., ed. by the Carl Diem Institut (Cologne 1977).
2. Carl Diem, *Ewiges Olympia. Quellen zum olympischen Gedanken* (Minden 1948); also his *Olympische Flamme*, vols. 1–3 (Berlin 1942), and *Ein Leben für den Sport. Erinnerungen aus dem Nachlaß*, ed. by the Carl Diem Institut (Ratingen 1974).
3. Avery Brundage, *Die Olympischen Spiele* (Stuttgart 1971); also his *Die Herausforderung*, trans. from American MS (Munich 1972), and *The Avery Brundage Collection 1908–1975* (Schöndorf 1977).
4. J. Moltmann, *Theology of Play*, trans. R. Ulrich (New York 1972) (= *Theology of Joy*, London 1973); trans. also into Dutch, French, Spanish, Italian, Portuguse, Japanese and Korean.

Thomas Ryan

Towards a Spirituality for Sports

THEOLOGY IS classically defined as 'faith seeking understanding' and is perhaps primarily seen in terms of *intellectual* understanding. I am going to confine my reflections to that realm of theology which relates to the patterns of behaviour which give concrete expression to one's faith: spirituality. Spirituality covers what the Fathers of the Church regarded as mystical theology, ascetic discipline and teaching on prayer. It takes in the relationship between prayer and conduct, and may be said to represent the spiritual aspect of our human striving for fulfillment in God.

The approach to sport in this essay is the same as that of the American philosopher William James to religion: through experience. The real backbone of the religious life, said James, is *experience*. No *philosophy* of religion, he contended, could begin an adequate translation of what goes on in the single private human being.

From the outset, let me say that I recognise the distinction between 'sports' and 'fitness or recreational activities'. In this distinction, sport pertains to competition sold as a commercial commodity, professionalism, perfecting the art form for its own sake. It involves fitness activities, but is not done primarily for fitness benefits or recreation. Two people may be playing tennis: one is preparing for the Davis Cup and is perfecting his play at the net; the other is playing just for the exercise, for the fun of it. The first is engaged in 'sport', the second in fitness activity or athleticism. I recognise that there is an important distinction between the two, even though in this essay I use the terms interchangeably.

Both sports and fitness activities are important for the individuals involved and for society. It is the duty of theology to make us aware of the deepest roots and implications of our activities.

The values reflected in sports make them more than pleasant diversion and recreation. If exercise can help us blow off angry steam, soothe jangled nerves, push along bulky food, teach us to respect and co-operate with others, and smile at the limits with which we discover our bodies are laden, then we can call exercise a faithful friend and should speak more of its holiness, of how it contributes to our spiritual growth.

The human qualities underlying athletic activities are the same as those underlying spiritual life activities. Discipline, dedication, enthusiasm, and perseverance are a few of those human qualities so evident in our play. They are the same ones that will get us out of bed at dawn to meditate, or enable us to protect fifteen minutes a day for the Word of God. The 'raw material', *i.e.* the virtuous quality, is the same. The difference is in its application. Millions of people have the raw material and only apply it in one direction, *i.e.* sports, when the same basic human virtues at work there could also be bringing them rich spiritual experience.

People usually associate asceticism with fasting and doing penance, but it essentially means *the artful shaping of a material*. The spiritual person is ascetic precisely because the spiritual person is the one who is interested in and dedicated to the artful handling of the world, the artful shaping of one's self, and the artful forming of one's life into something beautiful for God.[1] This artful fashioning of life seldom results from coercion or regimentation. It is best achieved by virtue of spontaneous desire and passionate pursual—qualities embodied in peoples' approach to play.

Thus, soccer and basketball and cycling can be disciplines of the spiritual life, too, inasmuch as they help provide one's character and personality with qualities that also lend themselves to the spiritual life ('grace builds on nature'). Through skiing, rock climbing, and white-water rafting, one learns how to deal with and overcome fear and anxiety. Through running, swimming, or rowing long distances one develops endurance and will power and learns how to deal with boredom. Through golf one can practise intense concentration and subtle control. Team sports can teach us the value of co-operation.

Discipline, freely chosen, fully experienced, is one of those transformational elements that has been neglected and even denigrated by our present culture. The practice of a spiritual discipline—any concentrated effort to create some inner and outer space in our lives so we may listen with attentive ears to the small, gentle voice of God (1 Kings 19:9–13)—is necessary. Meditation can be such a discipline, but so can running; both prevent the world from filling our lives to such an extent that there is no place left to listen. Further, if an activity is good for one's body, it is also good for one's spirit. There is only one seamless personality to which every benefit resounds.

Other examples of the constant interchange between bodily activities and spiritual benefits: sports set in motion our mental faculties of attention, observation, analysis, order, judgment, and evaluation. We'll need all of these qualities finely honed if we are to live as a Christian and discern gospel values in the midst of a secular society that seems little inclined to recognise God.

Fitness activities will contribute to the building of one's character through self-awareness and self-control, knowledge of one's own limitations, endurance, perseverance in effort, and determination to succeed. No Christian can journey through life without these qualities. They will enable us to get back up on our feet when we have fallen, knowing that we are forgiven, and that we can do nothing without God's help.

Athletics contribute to our social education, cultivating in us a spirit of mutual assistance, conscience, justice, respect for the other, submission to the rules, co-operation, sharing, and fellowship among people who share the same experience. This sense of team work is indispensable in responding to God's call. We are called to come to God *together*, not alone.

Most important, the experience of worry-less freedom that is ours in play reminds us that salvation is God's free gift. When we play, we knock out that deadly serious attitude towards life and leave it lying somewhere amidst the scattered bowling pins or unconscious on the bottom of the swimming pool. We do not always have to be achievers in life. We can also be a celebrator of what is given. When we lose our capacity for play, we lose our capacity for 'useless' presence to the Divine. This capacity is central to prayer which is essentially presence simply open to Presence.

One contribution of contemporary Christians to society would be the preservation and development of the play elements of sport. Churches should encourage play on all levels as part of their mission of evangelisation in contemporary society. If not from the Church, from what quarter can we hope for support in diminishing our idolatrous attachment to work? Allowing the spirit of play to enter into all levels of life is an integral part of the Christian mission to society.

Where modern society wants to move us more towards machines, sports bring us back toward people. Where modern society breeds individualism, play fosters socialisation. Where modern technology makes it easier for us to be passive, play summons us to be active. Sports gather us together in solidarity, counterbalancing some of the individualistic, self-serving tendencies fostered by contemporary society.

All of these points represent links between sports and our spiritual lives. Each one of them could be further developed, but I would like to focus on one quality in particular that I believe is the essential link between the world of athleticism and the world of the spirit: awareness. Its critical importance derives from the fact that experiencing is our fundamental activity; the quality of our lives in fact depends on the quality of our experiencing. And the ability to be *aware* is at the heart of the process of experiencing. Living with greater focus, with a heightened sense of awareness, makes all things new and fresh in our experience.

What does this have to do with our 'spirituality'? Let us begin with the word 'spiritual'. When people say 'spiritual' they mean a great variety of things, so we have to ask ourselves what we mean by spiritual. Since it comes out of the biblical vocabulary, going back to *spiritus* in Latin and *pneuma* in Greek and *ruach* in Hebrew, we have to ask ourselves what it means in a Western context. It means *aliveness*. Spiritual means alive— super-alive, if you want. That you have not yet died is not sufficient proof that you are alive. Aliveness is measured by degrees of *awareness*. And the spiritual work of our time is the task of making things alive, of heightening awareness.

The essential connection between spirituality and sports or fitness activity is that athletics make one alert, mindful, aware—which are precisely the qualities which make every activity become full of presence. To be sure, athletic activity is not the only way to heighten awareness; people do this in many different ways—through music, art, sex, meditation, and so on. My purpose here is simply to speak to how athletics does contribute to greater alertness, mindfulness, awareness.

This is the central idea behind *Zen and the Art of Archery*.[2] The 'art' of archery does not refer to the ability of the sportsperson, which can be more or less controlled by bodily exercises, but an ability whose origin is to be sought in spiritual exercises and whose aim consists in hitting a spiritual goal. When the pupil risks getting stuck in the mire of his achievement, the master reminds him that all right doing is accomplished only in a state of true selflessness, and that more important than all outward works is the inward work which he has to accomplish if he is to fulfill his vocation as an artist. 'A good archer,' the master tells him, 'can shoot further with a medium strong bow than an unspiritual archer can with the strongest. It does not depend on the bow, but on the presence of mind, on the vitality and awareness with which you shoot.'[3]

This 'right presence of mind' of which the Zen master speaks is charged with spiritual awareness, intuitive awareness, and is an essential quality for prayerful living. In other words, Mindfulness makes for wholehearted living which is prayerful living.

The spiritual life is not a question of *making* us religious, but helping us realise that we already *are* religious in the depths of our being. The work of the spiritual life is to become more *aware* of it. Spirituality does not just bring a set of practices, a booklet of prayers, or a system of doctrine to daily life. It brings an awareness to the people and events of each day that reflects their essential sacredness. There is no special designation of only certain times or kinds of activity as 'holy', but an appreciation for the holiness of life and the goodness of creation. The spiritual aspects of existence is not experienced as something to 'add on' but is integral to and at the very heart of our lives. The Kingdom of God, in other words, is not a place, but an *experience* of intensity, quality, depth, ecstacy.

Let us briefly examine the relationship of awareness to prayerfulness. People who are in the habit of saying prayers at certain set times often discover that their moments of genuine prayer are precisely at those times when they are not 'saying prayers'. In fact, they may not even recognise their most prayerful moments as prayer. Others who never say formal prayers are nourished by moments of deep prayerfulness. Yet, they would be surprised to learn they are praying at all.

Suppose, for example, that you are reciting psalms. If all goes well, this may be a truly prayerful experience. But all doesn't always go well. While reciting psalms, you might experience nothing but a struggle against distraction. Half an hour later you are out for a jog on your favourite woodland trail. Now, suddenly the prayerfulness that never came during the prayers overwhelms you. You come alive from within. Your heart expands and embraces those translucent autumn leaves, those explosions of colour in the blossoms looking up at you from the grass, those people whom you meet along the trail. Or when you are swimming, there comes the moment when you cannot separate the water from yourself, and in a rush of gratefulness your heart celebrates this belonging together. As long as this lasts, everything has meaning, everything makes sense. You are communicating with your full self, with all there is, with God. Which was the real prayer, the psalms or your run through the woods? The ripe fruit of a genuinely prayerful experience is to bring back into the humdrum routine of our daily lives, not just the *thought* of God, but the *awareness* of God's presence.[4]

In reflecting on what makes our prayers prayerful, David Steindahl-Rast notes that 'sooner or later we discover that prayers are not always prayer. That is a pity. But the other half of that insight is that prayer often happens without any prayers. And that should cheer us up. Especially if we want to do what Scripture tells us to do and "pray continually" (Luke 18:1)'.[5] When the apostle Paul speaks about prayer, he does not speak about prayer as a part of life, but says it is *all* of life. He does not mention prayer as something we should not forget, but claims it is our ongoing concern. He does not exhort his readers to pray once in a while, regularly, or often, but without hesitation admonishes them to pray constantly, unceasingly, without interruption. For Paul, praying is like breathing. 'Pray constantly, and for all things give thanks to God, because this is what God expects you to do in Jesus Christ' (1 Thess. 5:17–18).

If 'praying continually' meant saying prayers uninterruptedly day and night, there is no way we could fulfill that invitation. If, on the other hand, prayer is simply communication with God through a heightened sense of awareness and presence to the Mystery who is present to us in each moment, it can go on continually. In peak moments of awareness this communication will be more intense. At other times it will be low key. Through a prayerful attitude, every activity can and should become prayer.[6]

Those of us who have been saying prayers every day for many years and who have been trying to make our prayers truly prayerful should have some answer to the question: 'What is it that makes prayers prayerful?' When we try to put into words what the secret might be, words like mindfulness, full alertness, and wholehearted attention suggest themselves. These are not only the attitudes that make prayer prayerful, but are attitudes required for athletic activity.

This is the vital connection that enables me to assert that there are many spontaneous moments of prayer in fitness and sporting activities. On one occasion while alpine skiing in the Canadian Rockies, I took a lift up to the very peak of the mountain and crossed over the top, gliding down into a back bowl. Within seconds I discovered myself completely alone in a vast expanse of space, with the jagged peaks towering above me, no other skier in sight and not a sound to be heard. I stood transfixed for a long while. The Scriptures use the word 'theophany' for such moments when the Divine is experienced breaking through and transfiguring natural events with a sense of the sacred. When I finally pushed off with my poles, I did so slowly and deliberately, with a sense of one touched by the Holy and visited with awe. Even now, years later, I can recall that experience and those feelings with astonishing clarity. I have no other word for it than mystical—a level of experience to which I am convinced we are all called. It is primarily a question of refining our inner and outer senses to the presence of the Holy, daily in our midst.

Why do athletes have a special aptitude for a rich spiritual experience? Because the dancer or gymnast or crew member knows things through, with, and in her enfleshed spirit that pass the rest of us by. For she has exercised her embodied self, while we have lounged and loafed. Our range of humanity, of awareness, is constricted. The potential God gave us is unplumbed. How could we not know we were supposed to become lithe and well-conditioned? What master craftsman could make such a marvel as the human body and not be disappointed when we allow it to rust?[7]

Where shall we start in cultivating this heightened sense of awareness? I can only suggest that we begin with what comes easiest. For athletes, it is their times of play. These are the experiences that they tend to tackle with spontaneous mindfulness, so that without an effort their whole heart is in it. And because their heart is in it, they find a meaning in it which fulfills. It goes without saying that sportspersons may pursue several objectives at the same time and these objectives need not be mutually exclusive because they are located at different levels of one's consciousness.

What is asserted here is that, on one level, these are moments of intense prayerfulness, though we might never have thought of them as prayer. They show us the close connection between praying and playing. Being 'spiritual' is not essentially a question of religious beliefs but of being very alive, very tuned-in and aware. These moments of focused awareness are samples of what prayer is meant to be. If we could maintain this inner attitude, our whole life would become prayerful. The task is to approach not only some but all situations in this attitude of mindfulness. As one maxim puts it: 'Do the very next thing you have to do. Do it with your whole heart and find delight in it.'

Sporting people have the opportunity of already knowing what it is that they want to make their own in a more sustained way; they know it from the inside, they know it from those sporting moments when their hearts are wide awake. It is to these peak experiences of the heart that we must go back if we want to learn to *live* prayerfully. When religious traditions speak of the divine life within us, they refer, implicitly at least, to our high points of wakeful awareness, to our mystical experiences. Let us not shy away from that word, for we are all called to mysticism. A mystic is not a special kind of human being; rather, every human being is a special kind of mystic.

When the 'mental' aspects of sports are given more attention and when the 'mystical' elements are allowed to rise from the underground to full awareness, then the transformational elements in the experience of athleticism will become more commonly recognised.

Those participating in fitness activities tend to assume that the quality of their experience is the result of what is happening to them, so they put a lot of emphasis on the externals. They look for better skis, better running shoes, better racquets, better skates, better gloves, better clubs. Although we can alter our lives by changing our environment, most significant changes occur when we find effective ways to change our inner landscape.

Athletics, in addition to flattening one's stomach and slimming one's hips, can change the way one lives and provide foundational experiences for lasting transformation of consciousness. The intensity of the experience, the intricacy of the relationships, the total involvement of the body and senses, all come together in sports to create the precondition for those quality experiences that culture calls 'paranormal' or 'mystical'.

Such experiences will only surprise those who see the world without benefit of an incarnational spirituality. The constant points of reference must be that we are created in God's own image, and that God has become flesh that we might become like God. No matter how fallen we are, redemption and transformation are readily and presently available. Everything in creation carries the message, most of all this flesh which harboured the Word itself.

In that event, the world quite literally became the body of God. Ever afterward, we have no grounds on which to dismiss this world as some second-rate practice field for the real life in heaven. The Incarnation states that there is no practice and that nothing is second-rate. Life in this world is the life of God.[8]

The more attuned we become to the flesh God embraced and in which God dwells, exulting in its harmony, strength, and flexibility, learning how to bear its tensions and sufferings gracefully, the more we glorify its Creator, the One who also chose to call it 'home'.

The Ultimate Athlete is, in George Leonard's definition:

–one who joins body, mind and spirit in the dance of existence;
–one who explores both inner and outer being;
–one who surpasses limitations and crosses boundaries in the process of personal and social transformation;
–one who pays the larger game, the Game of Games, with full awareness, aware of life and death and willing to accept the pain and joy that awareness brings;
–one who, finally, best serves as model and guide on our evolutionary journey.

This ideal, which must remain tentative and open-ended, does not exclude anyone because of physical disabilities. In fact, the overweight, sedentary, middle-aged man or woman becomes a hero just by making a first laborious, agonizing circuit of the track. Six months or a year later, many pounds lighter, eyes glowing, that person may provide a model of the potential that exists in every one of us. To go a step further: if that person, recognizably transformed in body, mind and spirit, takes this experience as the impetus for further explorations and boundary

crossings and the heightening of awareness, then he or she must be said
to have embodied the ultimate athletic ideal.[9]

Notes

1. Francis Bauer, *Life in Abundance: A Contemporary Spirituality* (New York 1983),
   p. 256.
2. Eugen Herrigel, *Zen and the Art of Archery* (New York 1983).
3. *Ibid.*, p. 80.
4. David Steindahl-Rast, *Gratitude, the Heart of Prayer* (New York 1984), p. 40.
5. *Ibid.*, pp. 40, 41.
6. *Ibid.*, pp. 39–59.
7. John Carmody, *Holistic Spirituality* (New York 1983), pp. 77, 78.
8. Bauer, *op. cit.*, pp. 84, 85.
9. George Leonard, *The Ultimate Athlete* (New York 1974), pp. 287, 288.

Hans Lenk

Sport Between Zen and the Self

The experience of 'flow' and the meditative dimension in sport

'WITH EVERY run you come to live through your own experience', opines Fred Rohe, a Zen guru of running. Whereas this sentence may simply be understood in its everyday meaning, other statements about a meditative philosophy of life are highly stylised:

> The experience of meditative running has shown me that it is possible to live my whole life meditatively. And it seems to me that I ought to learn how to live like this, because for me it means that I am calm, courageous, alert and full of energy; in this way I am conscious of every instant of life, until one day life in this body ends. Thus a viewpoint of meditative running is the joy of the moment, another viewpoint is the learning process, in which running serves only as an allegory for everything that life means. . . . There is no standard to attain, no victory, only the joy of life in the dance of your run. There is joy in every life; only in the moment—now. So you too will know in the flow of your dance: You cannot run for a future reward; everything that is yours you receive *now*!

Zen in sport is high fashion; yoga techniques are incorporated in mental training. The Tao and the art of inaction, of the flowing, adaptive refusal to be frustrated, are recommended to sportsmen and women as well.

Zen culture in particular found its way into fashionable training courses which deviated from traditional patterns of teaching, after Eugen Herrigel's pioneer work *Zen in der Kunst des Bogenschiessens* (ET *Zen and the Art of*

Archery, 1983). In this process Suzuki's reference to Zen teaching in the old Japanese art of swordfighting played a special part. The basic idea is: 'Technical practice by itself is not enough' as Suzuki repeatedly emphasises. A master must have reached the ultimate stage of mental practice, namely the condition of the 'Not heart', an ego-less condition, 'non reflection' 'absence of thought', complete absorbtion and reflectionless immersion in the practice: 'No definition, no "observance", no consideration and no distinction'. It is not 'purely technical mastery of an art' that makes a real master. 'Rather he must simultaneously have penetrated deep into the spirit of the art. But this spirit is not grasped until his heart is in complete harmony with the principle of life itself, that is to say when he reaches the mysterious condition of the soul which is called ... "absence of consciousness" ... At this point every art flows into Zen': into an 'unmoved comprehension', 'a kind of unconscious knowing', an intuitively experienced non-conceptual illumination:

> If this be applied to championship in the art of swordfighting, the highest degree of consummation is reached as soon as your heart is no longer concerned as to how the opponent is to be hit, and yet knows how to wield the sword in the most effective manner, when you are face to face with him. You simply floor him and do not consider that you have a sword in your hand and that somebody is facing you. No longer is there any thought of I and you—all is emptiness, the opponent, you yourself, the flashing sword and the sword arm; indeed, even the thought of emptiness is no longer there. From such absolute emptiness arises the most wonderful display of action ... And the same thing holds true of dancing. You simply take your fan in your hand, put your best foot forward and glide around. But if you are obsessed with how to move your arms and legs correctly, your heart is preoccupied and your dance goes to pieces. Complete abandonment means an entire forgetfulness of the ego and everything connected with it,

as Suzuki quotes from the letter of the classical master Takuan about combining Zen with the art of sword-fighting.

The sentences about dancing already contain the teaching of Kleist's 'Marionette theatre': conscious attention to the movement destroys its graceful perfection. The secret teachings of the schools of combat, the Japanese combat schools after Musaki contain the following short verse:

Even the tiger finds no place to sink his claws

Into a soul untouched by thought and agitation

Even before the fight begins
One alone is the victor,
He who is unmindful of his ego,
And dwells in primal freedom from the 'I'.

Reununciation of the ego, complete surrender to the flow of the action and practice, practice, practice is also the only way in which Herrigel learns archery after half a decade. 'You must learn how to wait properly' said the master archer to the neophyte Herrigel.

And how is that learned?

By getting free from yourself, by leaving yourself and everything that is yours so decisively behind that nothing more of you remains than tautness without intention. This condition, in which no longer is anything definite thought, planned, striven for, desired or expected, which does not aim in any particular direction and yet which knows from an indwelling plenitude of power that it can do possible and impossible deeds—this condition, fundamentally intention-free and ego-free, is said by the master to be really 'spiritual'. It is fact laden with mental alertness and hence is also known as 'true presence of the spirit'.

Herrigel gradually learns

to dance the measure without bow and arrow, so that after only a few steps we felt ourselves to be unusually concentrated, the more so the more determinedly we remembered to assist the process of concentration by an easily induced bodily relaxation. Then when during the lesson we again took up bows and arrows, these quiet exercises had such abundant after-effects that we then slid effortlessly into the position of the 'spiritual present'.

This art of quiet acceptance, the waiting, the renunciation of self, in which I, you and things, master and not-master no longer appear to be separated, 'is transmuted into Zen as motionless movement, dance without dancing' and changes people in the very depths of their being.

Bow and sword are not instruments of victory, are not weapons, but, according to Suzuki 'objects of enthusiasm'. He detects this intuitive knowledge, this ego-less condition, also in the description of a bullfight by the bullfighter Belmonte: 'With the last bull I succeeded for the first time in my life in giving myself up body and soul to the pure joy of the fight, without any consciousness of the spectators ... I was so intoxicated, so beside myself, that I hardly noticed it'—not even when he sustained a wound.

Durkheim emphasises that practice is not a means of achieving an objective, a road to outward success or victory, but that it leads people towards themselves, and is a road to self-realisation: 'Practice ceases to be simply a means of sharpening a skill. It becomes a way to help oneself or the other person to break through to being or to have it become a configuration in the world. So understood, practice becomes a medium of all true personal guidance.'

'One day the master shouted at the instant at which my shot sped', writes Herrigel (pp. 75ff., 74, 77), 'It is there! Bow down!' The master, who in the darkness had put the first arrow in the centre of the bullseye, the second in the recess of the first arrow, splitting it and hitting the bullseye next to it, says: 'I at any rate know it was not "I" who should be credited with this hit. "It" shot and made the hit. Let us bow down before the target as before Buddha!' 'Do you now understand', the master once asked after a particularly good shot, 'what "it" means: "It" shoots, "It" makes a hit?'

The new Zen interpretation in sport has become the fashion. Gallwey has written books about the 'inner game of tennis', Rohe about 'the Zen of running'. Others would like to use Zen in cross-country skiing (Blackburn et al.), as top skiers nowadays do. Even training for American football and in other varieties of sport is subjected to the fashion for Zen (Shaw, Sekida). Leonard cites several cross-country skiers, golfers, basketball and football players as well as the Atlantic flier Charles Lindbergh, who have experienced the ego-less condition of extreme concentration, akin to dreaming. From his own experiences in Aikido, a Japanese sport of self-defence, and in tennis he speculates about a 'body of energy in action' of the athlete, and argues for an enlargement, a making flexible and developing multiplicity of consciousness in training for sports. He even speaks about a 'flow of energy' and with his tennis trainer about 'tennis flow'. Life itself becomes for him a great game of flowing, the 'game of games' which all can play: 'Everyone is a potential athlete'. The reward, he holds, is in the game itself and in perceiving it. 'In the final analysis running is its own reward', and this is true of all sports. Running, he thinks, is rooted in myth; it re-enacts a simpler form of living and confirms our kinship with other mammals; it challenges us to live our lives with the utmost loveliness: 'Our forebears ran after food and love': the mythical huntress Atalante could 'only be won by those, whether men or gods, who could overtake her'.

Leonard sees the 'mythical quality' of sport everywhere, 'the game-like essence of human existence' in the game of life itself—in the unusual, but also in the usual. The 'ultimate', the great athlete ('The Ultimate Athlete'), a 'pattern and image, must remain mythical', represents a universally valid 'ideal', in which body, intellect and soul are united 'in the dance of existence' which 'overcomes boundaries' and explores both inner and outer being.

On a somewhat more modest level we can also note that sport is an aid to self-exploration, enabling the limits of physical and psychic endurance to be probed. In sport people 'can live out their search for excitement, challenge and risk by intentionally setting conditions which they then try to overcome. Human beings love to feel themselves to be competent and self-determined—this is one of the reasons why they look for challenges, in order to overcome them. To be, or to feel, capable of overcoming and mastering these challenges is a source of great satisfaction.' Orlick continues by saying that in view of the 'delicious uncertainty, the experience itself becomes the goal': 'Each one seeks his/her own level of challenge and achievement.' In torrent canoeing 'one not only masters a river, one experiences it': 'The calculated risk, the feeling of significance in the moment, the intensity of the experience enables one to emerge from the experience released and exhilarated and somehow enriched. It is more a quest for self-fulfilment than a pursuit of victory over others or over the river. Many kinds of sport can be viewed in this way'. 'Sport is a means of access to a sense of purpose and constant challenge and also a range of emotions that can only with difficulty be experienced elsewhere.'

Mallory, the legendary climber of Mount Everest in the 1920s, who remained on the mountain without anybody ever knowing whether he 'conquered' it, 'used climbing as a means of introspection, the exploration of his own "soul", his reactions, and especially of the relationship between feeling and muscle coordination'. Speaking about climbing Everest, Mallory said: 'Whom have we conquered? Nobody except ourselves. Have we won a kingdom? No and yes. We have gained an ultimate satisfaction and accomplished a fateful task. To struggle and to understand—the latter is never possible without the former'.

Without the dramatic highlights of the fashion for Zen, the behavioural scientist Csikszentmihalyi describes the inner shape and intrinsic satisfaction of activities that are purely ends in themselves, sought for their own sake or on account of the experiences bound up with them, often seemingly even with symptoms of addiction. Csikszentmihalyi characterises the 'holistic experience felt by people when acting with complete abandon as *flowing*'. The person is aware of his or her actions, but not of this awareness itself and not of a separation between the deed and the self; attention is centred on a limited area of delight; the person forgets him/herself, loses self-consciousness; clear objectives are clearly responses to the actions. The person controls his/her actions and the environment. The experience of flow arises from the process and is not dependent upon the result or observation. According to Csikszentmihalyi the discovery of a novum, the acceptance and probing of a challenge, problem-solving and the confrontation of personal skill and capability with 'physical or symbolic occasions of action' are characteristic of actions which can lead to the experience of flow. This experience can for example similarly occur in utterly absorbing occupational work, in creative work, but also for example with surgeons.

The conventional distinction between work and play ceases to apply. In the flow situation the actors 'concentrate their attention on a restricted area of attraction, forget personal problems, lose the sense of time and of their own presence, feel themselves to be competent and in control of themselves and have a sense of harmony and union with their surroundings'. Even with an activity that may give rise to the experience of flow, that experience is not accessible to everybody, and certainly not at all times. Yet it can also arise even with everyday actions as 'micro-flow'.

In addition to rock dancing, mountain climbing in particular—not the spectacular scaling of peaks, which would be an achievement attracting outward recognition—is investigated as an example of a sporting activity that can lead to rhythmical 'flow'.

Rock climbers interviewed by Csikszentmihalyi have reported that recollections and everyday problems fade away. Climbing 'becomes a world of its own, significant only for itself. It is an occasion for concentration. When you are in that situation, it is incredibly real, and supremely demanding. It becomes your whole world.' The world outside is 'shut out'. Climbing 'catalyses yourself . . . The movements . . . create one another'. 'It is an aesthetic dance.' The movements 'become one movement'. 'Action becomes fused with preparedness': 'It is a pleasant feeling of total integration. One becomes like a robot . . . no, more like an animal . . ., loses oneself in the kinaesthetic sensation . . . a panther, crouching and stretching on the rock.' One must

give oneself over entirely to climbing, fusing one's thinking with the rock. It is the ultimate in commitment in sport, in endeavours to participate. It is the Zen feeling, like meditation and concentration. One strives to direct the intellect to a single point . . . But when things become automatic, it is to some extent like a thing without an ego. Somehow the right thing gets done, without one's thinking about it or even doing anything . . . It just happens. And yet one is more concentrated.

Thus a man climbing the Matterhorn speaks of 'one of those rare moments of almost orgiastic unity, when I forgot myself and became lost in the action'.

The experience of flow is a strange one; it is experienced as exceptional, even as a religious activity full of transcendent meaning, with a symbolic content. For this reason many mountaineers (for example Mallory, the famous climber who was lost on Mount Everest) describe their sport as 'an art form'. 'Mountaineers are all artistic . . ., because they cultivate emotional experience for its own sake'. The symbolic meaning can include union with nature or self-interpretation or a critique of society. The ordinary standards of everyday life are, as it were, set aside; one is treading new ground not yet understood, which can be prestructured from the apparently unstructured experience of flow.

Csikszentmihalyi contrasts the experience of flow in mountaineering with experiences governed by the standards of ordinary life in the form of a list:

Intense concentration of the mind; clarity, the controllability of boundaries, demands, decisions and reflexes; fusion of action and perception, obvious danger underlying assessment and control; visions of rapture, health; timelessness; process orientation; the intrinsic goal that is its own reward; overcoming what is of no use; integration of mind and body; understanding of the true self, self-integration; direct and immediate communication with others in a similar position; true and complete dependence on others; a sense of the place of human beings in the universe; unity with nature; the agreement of psychology and ecology; the depth dimension 'up there'; encounter with ultimate questions.

In brief: In the experience of flow, climbing is experienced as the high point, the centre of life and as an activity of supreme value, which puts its impress on life and changes it, and completely 'unites body and soul with a feasible task which evaluates the ability and even the very existence of the actor' and as such is intrinsic reward enough.

Elsewhere I have also described such highly active trance conditions of an intrinsically motivating kind, as Gabler calls them, from my own experience in connection with a normal type of sport such as rowing. One's own life cannot be doubted or understood purely theoretically; it has both existential and aesthetic tonalities. Activity involves the whole person. The person *is* for the time the action, the flow of movement, in appearance its active centre.

Existentialist interpretations of sport (especially by Slusher) also refer to experiences of this kind, but they construe them precisely as the 'real thing', the 'authentic' existence or its expression. For Slusher sport is '*not* an extension of life, but rather an essential manifestation of the characteristics of existence': One is 'almost tempted to say that human beings are whole only when taking part in sport': 'Sport reveals the basis of human existence', it offers a chance to realise personal existence, because a person's own individuality and personality are expressed, the ego put to the test, discovered, enhanced, confirmed and made real, for existence and for growing out of everyday things, challenged to discover and prove itself. Slusher holds that inner authenticity and 'truth of being' can only be achieved through action and decision-making in which the existence of the person is challenged or even imperilled.

The risk of defeat or even of death in the context of a person's own actions and decisions heightens, indeed is a precondition of, 'inner authenticity', which *is* the personal being. 'Being is risk.' In types of sport involving risk human beings symbolically overcome death by overcoming the fear of death. 'Sport is good for the human person and challenges it to total commitment.' In sport not only 'emotional meaning' but also 'the sense of being' is enlarged and discovered. There is no running away or deceiving oneself in sport; in the risk of defeat or failure, standing one's ground, holding out, excelling, in overcoming false demigods the sportsman can exercise his or her freedom and arrive at 'authentic *being*' and 'true existence'.

It is a bold, passionate attempt to make sport the centre of being in existential construction. Slusher quotes a number of rather unconvincing personal testimonies from runners, a more substantial interpretation by a woman skier of her crucial fall at an Olympic heat—and particularly the views of a surfer, van Dyke:

Sportsmen go in for surfing in order to bolster their ego, to find a substitute for something that otherwise is missing in their life . . . They have a subconscious feeling that they are not doing anything that has a (definite) purpose. Human beings need an outlet that is satisfying to the ego. Surfing gives one a feeling of achievement, but the feeling is over in four seconds and then one has to start all over again. Riding the waves should be enjoyable, but it is not. It is absolute terror. Surfers in high waves . . . have to go out, to prove to themselves that they have no fear

... Once when my board broke up ... I knew that I was face to face with the ultimate ... And then I realized what an absolute farce it was. I still surf, because I am a slave to my culture. I am unable to transcend it.

Leaving aside the emotional content of the expressions, Slusher always talks about *sport*; the existential analysis is not—as it should be—related to different kinds of sport in different ways. Consequently the investigation remains too generalised and abstract, when it analyses aesthetic types of sport such as athletics with the same existential expressions of experience as it uses for hard sporting contests such as boxing or football. Moreover, Slusher does not define and describe 'authenticity' any more precisely, and so what is authentic remains obscure. There is also the question whether the existential visitation is so characteristic or whether in fact only a few athletes experience it. And why exactly should sport be *the* outstanding or only existential experience of the self? Should not also—as Csikszentmihalyi maintains—other activities which mediate extraordinary experiences be equally central to existential self-discovery?

The existentialist philosophy is radically individualistic; it almost completely ignores the essential significance of society and the social, which is also existential. This is also carried over into the way in which existential philosophy construes sporting activity. This also is too individualistic; at best it might apply to an individual sport. It needs to be supplemented by social aspects. It is true that Hyland has attempted to construe basketball according to Heidegger's philosophy, but it seems artificial to read the fear of death and premonitions of death, indeed any *fear* of existence, into that sport. The end of the game is not a symbolic end to existence. At most the 'being ahead of oneself' of the player in the game can be formally transposed. Hyland himself sees difficulties in transposing many concepts such as 'loneliness', 'anxiety', the general pronoun 'one' into the interpretation of the game of basketball.

The relationship to death, and being-ahead-of-oneself in Heidegger are characteristic of the fact that the existential philosophy is the Song of Songs of the individual. In it the aloneness of the person is emphasised to the utmost. There is no timelessness, no self-forgetfulness. It is characterised by radical individuality and aloneness of temporal experience. However, this is an entirely different concept from self-forgetfulness, timelessness, as described by Csikszentmihalyi in the experience of flow as in the case of mountaineering or rock dancing. And the same could be said of self-forgetfulness in the Zen experience. Despite the relationship to personal existence, and the shared emotional emphasis, the consciousness of the peak, the full commitment, the seriousness of the bond with the activity, the sense of adventure, the subjectivity and the lofty expressions found both in the Zen interpretation and in that of existentialism, there is nevertheless a fundamental difference: The construction placed upon it by existentialism is radically individualistic whereas Zen philosophy negates individuality. This being so, the two interpretations are irreconcilable or refer to different characteristics or phases of sporting activity.

This difference becomes clear in mountaineering, which is of course a particularly existentially tinged type of sport. In it the person and his/her existence are at stake, the nearness of death heightens the consciousness of individuality, of loneliness—at least insofar as boundary experiences of 'being held out into nothingness' are typical. The experience of flow in rock climbing neglects precisely this 'truth of being' in the existential risk, suppresses the danger that threatens and the individualistic experience of aloneness. In fact, the subject 'transcends individuality', or so Maslow thought.

When such incompatible approaches both claim to capture the summits of experience in sport, they cannot be of universal validity; they are one-sided or restricted to different peaks. Yet they all have something plausible about them: the completeness of the commitment in sport at the top, the constant risk of failure, the demand upon the person and the intellect, the almost complete concentration on the sport—all of this makes world class sport appear to athletes as vitally important. It is more than the 'most important non-essential in the world' (Peets). The training, the motivation, the expenditure of strength and time nowadays require top grade sportsmen and women to make sporting achievement a 'main aim' for a large span of their lives, one on which they depend with all their thoughts, their experiences—as it were with every fibre of their being. They live in sport, or think they live only in sport. Sport means more to them than just sport. This paramountcy of sport, imagined yet experienced as 'real', and the importance of basic physical and mental health do in fact confer on the sporting life of many a first class sportsman and woman an existential tinge with heightened concentration on the ego and a sharper emphasis on worldly things.

Over against this stands the experience of flow which has been described, with its ego-lessness, timelessness and oneness with the environment. These however are individual peaks of timelessness and self-forgetfulness. The experiences of flow are individual exceptional happenings experienced as unique, which although they set their mark on the overall set and attitude towards the activity and person of the subject, and give it a special accent, cannot wholly comprehend it. Neither can the existentialist experience of detachment circumscribe everything in sporting experience and activity (it disregards the social dimension, as stated above, and also the rational dimension).

The differing approaches, then, provide only partial aspects. As such they are naturally of considerable, if limited, significance. Both should be stripped of their dramatic language, and of their claim to have a monopoly in the interpretation of sport. Both the Zen philosophy's interpretation and that of existentialism take flight into paradoxical descriptions such as 'artless art', 'danceless dance', 'motionless movement' or statements such as: in sport 'human beings transcend themselves and can potentially reemerge with self-discovery', the 'Now' is in sport 'more . . . than it is'; Slusher also emphasises 'that a person has to flee the real world and enter the artificial realm of sport in order to define his/her authentic being'. These dialectical approaches, formulated in paradoxes and contradictions, appear to reveal the inadequacy of language to convey what goes on in sport. Goethe's Faust expressed it better: 'If you don't feel it you will never attain it. If it does not press out of the soul . . .', and 'Feeling is all—name is but sound and vapour.'

But is language really too clumsy, is it an instrument incapable of conveying what is experienced in action? Surely the flow approach has succeeded in doing this, even if recourse is had to metaphor and the interviewees take refuge in similar paradoxical formulations.

At all events, common to all these approaches is that, as Csikszentmihalyi emphasises, they relate to 'significant challenges to the individual', 'creative discoveries or projections of a novum' and 'problems' and 'difficulties to be solved' in dealings with the unusual, challenges which can be overcome only by straining personal capabilities to the utmost in an inwardly satisfying treatment of the experience as an end in itself. The inseparability of action and the self, as was emphasised by mountaineers in Csikszentmihalyi's investigation is also expressed in the existentialist approach of self-transcendence and the self-forgetfulness of the Zen philosophy. The meaning, the real being, lies in action. The quasi-orgiastic emergency situation, the superelevated intensity of feeling, is also expressed in both these approaches. At the peak of the existential experience of feeling the most intensive self-awareness merges into self-forgetfulness in an experience akin to orgasm. After his world record-breaking throw the American weight-putter declared on television that he had experienced a veritable 'throwgasm'.

Juri Vlasov who won the heavy weightlifting class in 1960 (and who also wrote poems) described the experience of the supreme exertion in sport in these words:

When the blood is hammering in your head, suddenly there is a calm within you. Everything appears much clearer and whiter than before, just as if a big searchlight were directed at you. At such a moment you are convinced that you possess all the power in the world, that you could do anything, that you have wings. There is no more worthwhile moment in life than this moment (*Frankfurter Allgemeine Zeitung*, 3 August 1983).

In a certain sense these differing approaches are related. Training and technique are important, but they are not everything. The essential experience of life—expecially in conditions of extreme demand for achievement or intensity of action—cannot be reduced to those components. Freely chosen goals and intrinsic motivation, intensive experience of feelings, pleasure in successful activity, in the achievement of 'authenticity' (whether individualistic or exalted above self in the rhythm of 'flow')—all this can come about in the peak experience of sporting activity, as in experience of the game or of art or in other ecstatic experiences.

Can sporting activity such as Japanese swordfighting or the art of archery communicate intensive experiences which give these activities the joy of the extraordinary? 'Beyond boredom and fear', as Csikszentmihalyi entitled his book—and also beyond preoccupation and outward reward? For their adepts, all such activities that are ends in themselves are their own reward. In this way sporting activity, self-motivated and free from external goals can find its deeper meaning in the process and the experience, in full commitment.

'As long as you do not venture into the tiger's cave, you will never catch a tiger cub', said the Zen monk Yuan-Wu (according to Suzuki). and in Acts 26:24 we read: 'Too much study is driving you mad'. Is sport such a study?

Bibliography
Cranston, Toller, quoted in *Frankfurter Allgemeine Zeitung*, 3 August 1983.
Csikszentmihalyi, M., *Beyond Boredom and Anxiety* (San Francisco/ London 1975.)
Herrigel, Eugen, *Zen in der Kunst des Bogenschiessens* (Verlag O.W. Barth, Weilheim 1965).
King, Billie Jean, quoted in *Frankfurter Allgemeine Zeitung*, 3 August 1983.
Kleist, Heinrich von, 'Über das Marionettentheater', in Leonard, G., *The Ultimate Athlete* (New York 1974).
Orlick, Terry, *In Pursuit of Excellence* (Champaigne, Ill. 1980).
Rohé, Fred, *Zen des Laufens* (Oldenburg 1982).
Slusher, Howard, *Man, Sports and Existence* (Phildadelphia 1967).
Suzuki, D.T., *Zen und die Kultur Japans* (Hamburg 1958).
Wlassow, Juri, quoted in *Frankfurter Allegemeine Zeitung*, 3 August 1983.

Contributors

JOHN COLEMAN, SJ, was born in San Francisco in 1937. He holds advanced degrees in sociology from the University of California, Berkeley and did advanced study in theology at the University of Chicago. The author or editor of over ten books, he is the author of *An American Strategic Theology*. He serves as the editor-in-chief for the Isaac Haecker series in American culture and religion published by Paulist Press in the USA. He is currently Professor of Religion and Society at the Graduate Theological Union in Berkeley, California.

ROBERTO DAMATTA is the Reverend Edmund P. Joyce Professor of Anthropology, and senior fellow of the Kellogg Institute, University of Notre Dame. He is a Brazillian anthropologist educated at the Federal Fluminense University in Niteroi, Rio de Janeiro and Harvard University. He was a professor of anthropology of the Museu Nacional Federal University of Rio de Janeiro, in Brazil, and was the main person responsible for implementing the teaching and research of Social Anthropology both in Rio and in Brazil. His publications include: *Carnavais, Malandros e Heróis* (1979) (soon to appear in English) *O que faz o brasil, Brasil?* (1986), *A Casa & a Rua* (1987); *Universo do Carnaval* and *A Divided World: Apinayé Social Structure* (Cambridge, Mass. 1982).

SEAN FREYNE is professor of theology at Trinity College Dublin, specialising in early Christianity in its social and religious environment. His most recent book is *Galilee, Jesus and the Gospels. Literary Approaches and Historical Investigations* (Dublin/Philadelphia 1988). As a former All Ireland champion Gaelic footballer he has a keen interest in all sports and occasionally dabbles in sports journalism.

KLAUS HEINEMANN was born in 1937. His first doctorate was in political science, and he gained his qualification as a lecturer in sociology in 1968 at the Technische Hochschule in Karlsruhe. He has held professorships in sociology in the University of Trier from 1970 to 1981 and in Hamburg since 1981. His main interests are economic sociology and the sociology of organisations, and the sociology and economics of sport. Since 1978 he has chaired the academic advisory board of the West German Sporting Union.

BRUCE KIDD. A former Canadian Olympian in long distance running, Bruce Kidd writes and teaches about the history and politics of sport at the University of Toronto. His books include *The Political Economy of Sport* (1979), *Tom Longboat* (1980), and *Athletes Rights' in Canada* (1982) with Mary Eberts. He also directs the Olympic Academy of Canada, an annual workshop on the problems and prospects of the modern Olympic Movement conducted by the Canadian Olympic Association.

HANS LENK was born in Berlin in 1935. He studied philosophy, mathematics, sociology, psychology and the science of sport in Freiburg and Kiel. He is presently professor of philosophy at Karlsruhe University, professor of the scientific theory of the social sciences and planning science at the Faculté Européenne des Sciences du Foncier, Strasbourg. His publications include: *Zwischen Wissenschaftstheorie und Socialwissenschaft* (1986); *Zur Kritik der wissenschaftlichen Rationalitat*, ed., (1986); *Zwischen socialpsychologie und Sozialphilosophie* (1987); *Technik und Ethik*, co-editor, (1987); *Kritik der kleinen Vernunft* (1987).

DIETMAR MIETH was born in 1940. He studied theology, German language and literature, and philosophy. He has further degrees in theology (Würzburg 1968) and in moral theology (Tübingen 1974). He was professor of moral theology at Fribourg from 1974 to 1981, and he has been professor of theological ethics at Tübingen since 1981. His publications include: *Die Einheit von vita activa und vita contemplativa* (Regensburg 1969); *Dichtung, Glaube und Moral* (Mainz 1976); *Epik und Ethik* (Tübingen 1976); *Moral und Erfahrung* (Freiburg ³1983); ed.; *Meister Eckhart* (Munich ³1986); *Gotteserfahrung—Weltverantwortung* (Munich 1982); *Die neuen Tugenden* (Düsseldorf 1984); *Ehe als Entwurf* (Mainz 1984); *Arbeit und Menschenwürde* (Freiburg 1985); *Die Spannungseinheit von Theorie und Praxis* (Freiburg 1986).

JÜRGEN MOLTMANN was born in Hamburg in 1926 and is a member

of the Evangelical-Reformed Church. He studied at Göttingen, was professor at the Kirchliche Hochschule Wuppertal from 1958–63, at Bonn from 1963–67, and now holds a chair for systematic theology at Tübingen. He is president of the Gesellschaft für Evangelische Theologie. His publications include: *Prädestination und Perseveranz* (1961); *Theologie der Hoffnung*, 12th ed. 1985 (ET *Theology of Hope*, 10th ed. 1983); *Perspektiven der Theologie*, 1968 (ET [selections] *Hope and Planning*, 1971); *Der Mensch*, 4th ed. 1979 (ET *Man*, 1974); *Die ersten Freigelassenen der Schöpfung*, 6th ed. 1976 (ET *Theology of Joy*, 3rd. ed. 1982 [in USA as *Theology of Play*]); *Der gekreuzigte Gott*, 5th ed. 1986 (ET *The Crucified God*, 8th ed. 1985); *Kirche in der Kraft des Geistes*, 1975 (ET *The Church in the Power of the Spirit*, 2nd ed. 1981); *Zukunft der Schöpfung*, 1977 (ET *The Future of Creation*, 1979); *Trinität und Reich Gottes*, 2nd ed. 1985 (ET *The Trinity and the Kingdom of God*, 2nd ed. 1986); *Gott in der Schöpfung*, 3rd ed. 1987 (ET *God in Creaton*, 1985).

GUNTER PILZ was born in 1944, and holds a doctorate in philosophy and a diploma in sociology, having studied sociology, psychology and political economy. He is senior lecturer at the Institute for Sport Studies in the University of Hanover. He specialises in the study of violence in sport and society. He has produced reports for the West German Interior Ministry on 'Sport and Violence' (1981), 'The Presentation of Violence in Sport in the Media and its Effects' (1987), and 'Fan Culture and Fan Behaviour' (1988). His most recent book is *Die Welt der Fans. Aspekte einer Jugendkultur* (1988).

THOMAS RYAN, CSP, was born in Minneapolis, Minnesota (USA) in 1946 and ordained in the Paulists in 1975. He studied in the USA at Don Bosco College and the Washington Theological Union, and in Switzerland at the Ecumenical Institute at Bossey. He is director of the Canadian Centre for Ecumenism in Montreal, and editor of the international quarterly *Ecumenism*. His publications include: *Fasting Rediscovered: A Guide to Health and Wholeness for Your Body-Spirit* (New York 1981); *Tales of Christian Unity* (New York 1984; French translation: *Sur les Chemins de l'unité* (1985)); *Wellness, Spirituality and Sports* (New York 1986); and *A Survival Guide for Ecumenically Minded Christians* (1989).

NANCY SHINABARGAR was born in Los Angeles in 1956. She completed her undergraduate education in history and political theory at the University of California, Berkeley. She is currently a doctoral student in ethics and society at the Graduate Theological Union, Berkeley.

CONCILIUM

CONCILIUM

CONCILIUM 1988

All back issues are still in print: available from bookshops or direct from the publishers (£5.95/US$11.95/Can$12.75 excluding postage and packing).

T & T CLARK LTD, 59 GEORGE STREET EDINBURGH EH2 2LQ, SCOTLAND

SUBSCRIBE TO CONCILIUM

'**CONCILIUM** a journal of world standing, is far and away the best.'

The Times

'... it is certainly the most variegated and stimulating school of theology active today. **CONCILIUM** ought to be available to all clergy and layfolk who are anxious to keep abreast of what is going on in the theological workshops of the world today.'

Theology

CONCILIUM is published on the first of every alternate month beginning in February. Over twelve issues (two years), themes are drawn from the following key areas: dogma, liturgy, pastoral theology, ecumenism, moral theology, the sociology of religion, Church history, canon law, spirituality, scripture, Third World theology and Feminist theology (see back cover for details of 1989 titles). As a single issue sells for £5.95 a subscription can mean savings of up to £15.75.

SUBSCRIPTION RATES 1989

	UK	USA	Canada	Other Countries
New Subscribers	£19.95	$39.95	$49.95	£19.95
Regular Subscribers	£29.95	$49.95	$64.95	£29.95
Airmail		$67.95	$84.95	£39.95

All prices include postage and packing. **CONCILIUM** is sent 'accelerated surface post' to the USA and Canada and by surface mail to other destinations.

Cheques payable to T & T Clark. Personal cheques in $ currency acceptable. Credit card payments by *Access*, *Mastercard* and *Visa*.

'A bold and confident venture in contemporary theology. All the best new theologians are contributing to this collective summa'.

Commonweal

Send your order direct to the Publishers

T & T CLARK LTD

Publishers   *since 1821*

59 GEORGE STREET
EDINBURGH
EH2 2LQ
SCOTLAND

International Theological Conference

On the occasion of the 25th anniversary of CONCILIUM

from September 9–14, 1990, at the University of Leuven

THEME: ON THE THRESHOLD OF THE THIRD MILLENIUM

THE THEME of the conference is in three sections. The first will review the recent past of church and world and evaluate both positive and negative aspects.
Speakers: E. Schüssler Fiorenza and C. Duquoc

A more analytical and descriptive second section deals with the choice for life or death.
Speakers: J. Moltmann and D. Tracy

The third section especially involves the religious and theological manner of speaking about God and the coming kingdom of God as salvation and well-being of and for mankind.
Speakers: H. Küng and G. Gutiérrez

The lectures will be printed in advance in February 1990 in a special conference issue of CONCILIUM. This will allow emphasis during the actual conference to fall on group discussion and plenary meetings.

With this announcement CONCILIUM invites all those interested in the conference to take part in it as observers.

We would welcome your applications addressed to the General Secretariat of CONCILIUM, c/o Mrs. E. Duindam-Deckers, Prins Bernardstraat 2, 6521 AB Nijmegen, The Netherlands.

We can also supply information about inexpensive lodgings.

The registration fee for the conference is US $15.00

We would like to request that all Faculties and Institutes pin up a notice about this conference in a place appropriate to informing any interested visitors about it.
For this you can use a copy (enlarged) of the Announcement.